WINNING AT HOME

TIMELESS TRUTHS FOR LEADERSHIP AND GODLINESS IN THE HOME

DR. C.F. HAZLEWOOD

LUCIDBOOKS

Winning at Home

Timeless Truths for Leadership and Godliness in the Home

Published by Lucid Books in Houston, TX
www.LucidBooks.com

ISBN: 978-1-63296-923-1
eISBN: 978-1-63296-924-8

Special Sales: Most Lucid Books titles are available in special quantity discounts. Custom imprinting or excerpting can also be done to fit special needs. Contact Lucid Books at Info@LucidBooks.com

Contents

Introduction

In Colossians 3, the Apostle Paul offers a blueprint for harmonious relationships within the Christian household, emphasizing the unique responsibilities of each family member. This scriptural passage lays out the roles of wives, husbands, and children, giving guidance on how they are to interact and uphold their respective duties. These instructions, simple yet profound, serve as a roadmap for cultivating loving, respectful, and God-honoring relationships at home.

The family is one of the most foundational units in society, meant to be a source of support, love, and guidance. Paul's teachings in Colossians 3 resonate with timeless truth, shedding light on how individuals can contribute to a household environment that reflects God's love and grace. The responsibility for this lies with each member, and when these roles are embraced with humility, patience, and mutual respect, the household can become a place of growth and joy.

At the heart of Paul's message is the concept of love, which binds the family unit together in perfect harmony. This love, however, is not merely sentimental or superficial; it is a call to sacrificially seek each other's well-being. Each role—whether that of a wife, husband, or child—carries a sacred responsibility to foster this environment. Paul emphasizes that these roles should be approached with a mindset of service to one another, mirroring Christ's selfless love.

The purpose of this book is to delve deeply into the guidance provided in Colossians 3, exploring what it means to live out these roles practically. Each chapter will examine the responsibilities laid out for wives, husbands, and children, and offer insights into how these roles can be approached in a way that honors God and strengthens family bonds. Additionally, this book aims to address the challenges that modern families face in adhering to these roles and the practical ways they can cultivate the qualities Paul encourages love, patience, kindness, humility, and forgiveness.

For wives, Paul highlights the importance of respect and support within the marriage, underscoring how these actions can be an act of worship and service, both to God and their families. For husbands, the responsibility extends beyond mere provision; Paul calls them to lead with love, gentleness, and understanding, embodying the sacrificial love of Christ. For children, obedience to parents is framed as an act of honoring the authority God has placed in their lives, establishing a foundation of respect that will serve them well into adulthood.

As you journey through the pages of this book, may you find fresh inspiration to embrace the biblical vision for family life. It is an invitation to reflect on the ways we relate to each other, to learn from the wisdom of Scripture, and to seek God's guidance in transforming our households into reflections of His kingdom on earth. In doing so, we are not only fulfilling a call but also building a legacy of faith, love, and harmony that can inspire future generations.

Let us explore together how these age-old principles can find new life in our modern world, shaping families that stand firm in faith, love, and unity.

CHAPTER 1
Stewardship
The Family and Creation

Wives, submit to your own husbands, as is fitting in the Lord. Husbands, love your wives and do not be bitter toward them. Children, obey your parents in all things, for this is well pleasing to the Lord. Fathers, do not provoke your children, lest they become discouraged. Bondservants, obey in all things your masters according to the flesh, not with eyeservice, as men-pleasers, but in sincerity of heart, fearing God. And whatever you do, do it heartily, as to the Lord and not to men, knowing that from the Lord you will receive the reward of the inheritance; for you serve the Lord Christ. But he who does wrong will be repaid for what he has done, and there is no partiality.—Colossians 3:18–25

Within the context of Colossians and what has come before this passage, Paul has been talking about putting on the new man and taking off the old man. This relationship with the new man and the old man demonstrates what we should and should not do, what we should put on and what we should take off, and ultimately, how we should live. So, why does Paul jump straight into family relationships?

The reason is certainly that the closest relationships we have on this earth are with our family. And that is the first place where we wear our faith.

Unfortunately, sin has created problems in marriage and in the family. We see that in Colossians as well. Whether you are currently in a relationship or not, I hope this will be valuable information for you to understand the whole of Christian living.

Why are there problems in marriage? Why are there problems in relationships? To answer that, let's go back to the very beginning—to the book of Genesis.

The first thing we need to understand about the family is this: In the beginning, God created the heavens and the earth. And that tells us God puts Himself at the very beginning of the Bible, sovereign over all that is out there. God is our ultimate source of authority. He is the guide for all that we do in the Christian life. We relate back to God and what He has done. He sovereignly created the heavens and the earth. He also created man, unique and different.

> *Then God said, Let Us make man in Our image, according to Our likeness; let them have dominion over the fish of the sea, over the birds of the air, and over the cattle, over all the earth and over every creeping thing that creeps on the earth.' So God created man in His own image; in the image of God He created him; male and female He created them.*—Genesis 1:26–27

God created human beings, and He created a male and female, and He created them for a purpose and for a reason.

> *Then God blessed them, and God said to them, 'Be fruitful and multiply; fill the earth and subdue it; have dominion over the fish of the sea, over the birds of the air, and over every living thing that moves on the earth.*—Genesis 1:28

"God said"—you could preach an entire sermon on that statement. What is the importance of that? It's God establishing order. It's God providing guidance. It's God giving instruction. It's God putting Himself, rightfully so, in a position of sovereign and so can speak to His creation. He can speak to His creation because He brought His creation into existence. We are His handiwork. So we receive our orders from God.

These verses say God blessed them, and one of the first things God said to man and woman when He put them on earth was to have dominion over the creation. What does it mean to have dominion over the creation? What does that speak to us about?

Having dominion over creation means that God has put us as His authorities over all the earth. We're to have dominion, to control it, and manage it. We're to be stewards of the creation. A good biblical understanding of man's relationship to the creation is that man and, in particular, Christian men and women, are called to be environmentalists. I'm not talking about what has become the current definition of environmentalists, which is basically a form of terrorism in our country. I'm talking about true environmentalism. As a Christian, you should be concerned about the creation. You should want to make sure the creation is taken care of. Wherever you are, whatever you do, be a good steward.

What is a steward? It's someone who manages the affairs of another. So as stewards over the creation, we are to manage God's creation. The current concept of environmentalism comes from a non-Christian worldview, which we would refer to as a pantheist worldview.

What is pantheism? Pantheism is an Eastern belief that centers upon the idea that all of the created order is God, and we're all just elements of it. It's the view that we are equal in that. So, man is no more valuable than a fish; man has no more authority than a cow. There's just as much value in each one of them. But from God's perspective, man is a special order of creation in that He is created in the image and likeness of God. The rest of the creation is created by God, and man has been put in a position to manage that creation.

So, while we should be good, solid environmentalists from the standpoint that we manage God's creation, we should remember that animals and all of creation were given to us for our usage. And that is clear from Scripture.

Genesis 1 goes on to say, *And God said, 'See, I have given you every herb that yields seed which is on the face of all the earth, and every tree whose fruit yields seed; to you it shall be for food. Also, to every beast of the earth, to every bird of the air, and to everything that creeps on the earth, in which there is life, I have given every green herb for food;' and it was so.*

This tells us that in God's original creation, everything was vegetarian. Every man was a vegetarian, animals were vegetarians, and they all ate vegetables. It was not until after the flood when God re-established man on the earth, that He gave permission to eat meat. And so, man began to consume meat at that time. Prior to that, humans were vegetarian. So, we see that the heavens and the earth were created by God for His satisfaction, but He has put us over them to manage—or to be stewards of—that creation.

Finally, Genesis 1 ends by saying, *God saw everything that He had made and indeed, it was very good. So, the evening and the morning were the sixth day.*

If we move on to *Genesis 2:15*, it says, *Then the Lord God took the man and put him in the garden of Eden to tend and keep it. And the Lord God commanded the man, saying, "Of every tree of the garden you may freely eat; but of the tree of the knowledge of good and evil you shall not eat, for in the day that you eat of it you shall surely die.'*

In *Genesis 2:18*, God goes on to say, *It is not good for man to be alone.*

You may notice He said just before in Genesis 1:27 that He created a male and female. Then you get over to chapter two, and He is about to create a female? What is going on here?

That is Hebrew-style literature. God writes about His created order. Then, in Chapter Two, it is as if he opens a new window on a computer. He is opening up another window that will explain how He created man. He is just going into further detail in this new section. Moses wrote like that a lot. He'd often write a general premise statement, and then the next chapter or later on, boom. He'd expand that. He would open it up. So, what we're going to see is how man and woman came into existence. God put man in the garden to attend and keep it. He commanded him to take control of that garden, and He said not to eat from the tree of knowledge of good and evil.

Then in *Genesis 2:18*, the Lord God said, *It is not good that man should be alone. I will make a helper comparable to him.* That means one who comes alongside as a complement to him. Man and woman are both created in the image and likeness of God. Man and woman are co-regents over the creation. Man and woman were meant for marriage—to be together. And then, out of the ground, the Lord God formed every beast of the field, every bird of the air, and then brought in Adam to see what he would name them or call them. Once again, it is showing where Adam has authority over the creation. Naming the creation means he's in a position of authority, as it is understood in Hebrew. And whatever Adam called every living creature, that is its name.

Adam gave names to all the cattle, all the birds of the air, and every beast of the field. But for Adam, there was not found a helper comparable to him. And the Lord God caused a deep sleep to fall on Adam. While he slept, God took one of Adam's ribs and closed up the flesh in its place.

As a side note, you may have heard people say that women have one more rib than men. It's important to understand that God took one rib out of Adam and created a woman. The next man to come along was born. So, he would have all his ribs. Just like if I chop my hand off, my kids wouldn't be born without a hand. God took Adam's rib, and only Adam. As Christians, we don't want to fall for those kinds of things and repeat them without facts.

It Begins with Marriage

In verse 22, the Bible goes on to say, *Then the rib which the Lord God had taken from man, he made into a woman.* That word *made* means He fashioned a work of art; God shaped and sculpted a woman out of the rib and brought her to the man. What is a biblical basis for marriage? It's when God brings people together.

The emphasis for marriage is not finding a mate. But the emphasis for marriage should be asking ourselves, 'Am I the right mate?' Am I doing what's right? That's what you need to focus on. Don't worry about the other part—you take care of yourself. God will bring the right people together. That's what He does.

> *And Adam said, 'This is now bone to my bone and flesh of my flesh. She shall be called woman because she was taken out of man.' Therefore, man will leave his father and mother and be joined to his wife and they shall become one flesh. And they were both naked, the man and his wife, and they were not ashamed.*—Genesis 2:23–25

What does that tell us? God brings them together, and we see the three critical components for a marriage in this passage. The first of these three critical components is that a man will leave his father and mother. Marriage begins when one leaves their family and starts a new family unit. For a marriage to function well, you must leave your mother and father. That does not mean you don't get advice or guidance. Only a fool would ignore the wisdom of others. But it means you are starting your own family unit. You're breaking out of that family and starting your own.

The second part we see is where it says joined. The Old King James would use the word cleave. So, the second one is to be joined or cleave to his wife. That word means you stick like glue. It's a commitment and a relationship that has to be permanent. That is God's perfect plan for marriage. You become joined or glued together, and in the case of Adam and Eve, they became one flesh. God's math works like this: one plus one equals one.

Those are the three critical components of a marriage: leave, cleave, and become one. Man and woman together become one. What does that tell you? Man's purpose or God's purpose in a marriage is for a unified front with the husband and wife. A husband and wife are a team. They come together, they are joined together, they're in a solid relationship. That's the perfect relationship.

In the last verse, *Genesis 2:25*, it states, *'and they were both naked.'* And the man and his wife were not ashamed. They are together, they're one, a unified and bonded entity, and they are naked and not ashamed.

There is significance in that word being used because we know what happens next. Chapters 1 and 2 present a perfectly created world, a perfectly ordered universe. Then we come to Chapter 3, and we see the fall of man.

Now the serpent was more cunning than any beast of the field which the Lord God had made. And he said to the woman, 'Has God indeed said you shall not eat of every tree of the garden?' And the woman said to the serpent, 'We may freely eat the fruit of the trees of the garden, but the fruit of the tree which is in the midst of the garden God said, "You shall not eat it. Nor you touch it lest you die.'

And the serpent said to the woman, 'You will not surely die. For God knows in a day that you eat at your be open and you'll be like God, knowing good and evil.'—Genesis 3:1–3

And we know how the story goes.

Marriage and the Fall

When the curse came, whatever the serpent was, he was changed into what we call a snake today. He crawled on the ground. Prior to that, he was able to sit upright and communicate. We don't know what kind of being it was, but it no longer exists after the fall, because God transformed it into what we now call a snake. However, what we need to understand about this part of Scripture is what led to the fall. Casting doubt and uncertainty on the Word of God is what brought the fall.

The Word of God is extremely important. And when we deal with the family, we're not going to go by what society says. We're going by what the Bible says. Because God created man and woman in His image and His likeness. He made them a unified, united force to rule over the earth. We think about what an exalted position man had from God and the responsibility that man had to take control and charge over all of that. And from this scriptural view, we see where the evil attacks from—he casts doubt and uncertainty on the Scripture, and it throws this whole thing into chaos because they ate the fruit.

> *Then the eyes of both of them were opened, and they knew that they were naked; and they sewed fig leaves together and made themselves coverings. And they heard the sound of the Lord God walking in the garden in the cool of the day, and Adam and his wife hid themselves from the presence of the Lord God among the trees of the garden.*—Genesis 3:7–8

We see several things after the fall. Instead of being naked and unashamed, now they know they're naked, and they are ashamed—they're fearful of God. What you see in that passage is a natural progression of sin in the human being. And it is always the same. Sin leads to guilt, which our passage here refers to as nakedness. Nakedness, if not dealt with, will move to fear or anxiety, and then it will ultimately move to man fleeing or hiding. It's man trying to deal with his sin. And in this passage, man puts on fig leaves to cover his nakedness. What does that tell us?

Man does things to cover the guilt of his sin. It tells us man is fearful because of the guilt of this sin. We see where this comes from. What is sin? Sin is a lack of love toward God or toward your fellow man. God said, *If you love me, keep my commandments* (John 14:15). So, loving God is obedience to God, just as loving your fellow man is treating your fellow man in the way you'd want to be treated. You don't treat them in an unloving manner. The minute you do, the first thing that happens is guilt. You discover you're naked, and you become fearful, anxious, stressed, and then there's the fleeing mechanism.

They chose fig leaves. Some people choose an outburst of anger. Some people choose alcohol. Some people choose drugs. Some people choose overeating. There are all kinds of things you can do on the fleeing mechanism to compensate for the guilt and anxiety. That's a feel-good thing. That relieves the stress and pressure. That's the natural progression of it.

What we see from here is that it throws the whole marriage relationship into total chaos. God said that the day they ate from the tree, they would die. We go to the next chapter, and they're still alive. God goes up to them, and look what He says in verse 16 of chapter 3 of Genesis. *To the woman, He said, 'I will greatly multiply your sorrow.'*

What does that tell us? Well, after the fall, one of the things that's going to break this harmony up is that, as a result of sin, it says the woman is going to have sorrow. What does that mean? It means stronger emotions than a man. It doesn't say it's the man who will have sorrow—it is to the woman. Women tend to be more emotional than men. Women may be very facts-oriented, but they are generally also more emotional than men. There's nothing wrong with that, but we see that it's a result of the fall. From there, it shows that God multiplies her conception, which simply means that women are going to have more than one child.

In pain, you will bring forth children—(Genesis 3:16).

What is the significance of that? Why would God add pain to childbirth? Whenever you bring new life into the world as a woman, there is pain. That pain should remind you of the grace of God because God said that on the day they ate the fruit, He would kill them. You will die. Now they did die spiritually, but from their mindset, they believed they were going to die physically. That's what they thought. But pain and childbirth are a picture of God's grace.

New life comes, and with it, pain is associated. But that's not all He said. He says, *Your desire will be for your husband, and he shall rule over you* (Genesis 3:16).

That right there is the big problem in marriage. That word desire does not mean that a woman is going to have emotional desire for her husband. It does not mean that she's going to have physical desires for her husband. It doesn't mean that she's going to have sexual desires for her husband. That word desire is not a good word in Hebrew. The word desire means control. It means to dominate or to take charge of.

So the Lord said to Cain, 'Why are you angry? And why has your countenance fallen? If you do well, will you not be accepted? And if you do not do well, sin lies at the door. And its desire is for you, but you should rule over it.'—Genesis 4:7

What is He telling Cain? "Cain, sin is going to want to control your life, but you've got to take control of sin. Don't let sin run your life."

Just as with Cain and sin's desire over him, the woman's desire is over her husband. So, desire in that relationship means that the woman now, truly as a result of the fall, wants to control or have authority over the man. The word picture often used is that of an animal about to pounce on its prey.

I personally raise exotic poultry, and I've got some that I let run loose, but I feed them well. I throw out grain for them. And after I throw out the grain for them, then the local birds will come in. If they come in while those chickens are out, the chickens will chase them all. And those local birds will leave.

But after they finish their portion of the feed that I mix for them, those native birds move in. For instance, we have a lot of cardinals at my place.

One afternoon, I was sitting outside, looking at the little red cardinals that had come in. I counted 31 of them out there. They all landed out in my yard and were eating the leftover feed I'd tossed out there for my chickens. I also have two barn cats. The cardinals had their game plan, and their game plan consisted of getting the grain. Unfortunately, the cats' game plan was getting a cardinal. As I sat there, I watched the cardinals flock in there.

If you want to attract birds, put out food; the minute you start giving away free food, they just swarm.

Well, one barn cat got down by the edge of the yard and made a little move. She moved out there, low to the ground. I continued watching, waiting for the outcome to unfold. Birds can see in all directions with a flick of their little heads. And so they were looking at the cat, and the cat was looking at them.

That cat took some more steps and moved up, closing the distance. Now those birds have guards out there that are supposed to be like spies, but they get slack on guard duty, and they'll start cleaning their feathers and looking at the other birds and playing bird games. And that cat just continued to move in.

Well, eventually that cat pounced, successfully, and ate a cardinal. The cat was as happy as could be. And that is what the Word desire means. It means to creep up on something, and get it, and attack it. Because of the fall, the natural tendency of the woman is to want to control the man.

Look at the next part of that verse. *And he shall rule over you.*

That's not good either. As a result of the fall, the natural desire for the man is to dominate the woman. And because men are physically stronger than women in most cases, it is easier for a man to dominate their woman. Sometimes they dominate them physically, sometimes they dominate them verbally. Sometimes they dominate them emotionally. But whatever arena it comes in, it is a direct result of the fall. The man wants to push that woman down, and the natural tendency of that woman is to do what? Get him down. They pursue this instead of being one, united with a dominion over the creation.

What do we have now? We have two who are trying to control each other instead of controlling what God said to control. Sin throws a curveball in the middle of everything, and takes that beautiful relationship that God created, then it separates and divides that one. And then, instead of working together as co-regents over that creation, they start managing each other's lives.

I've seen it happen in marriages before, when women try to control the man and the man tries to control the woman. The man's control is usually more open than the woman's, but the woman's control tends to be more subtle. Both, however, are a manifestation of the flesh, and neither one of them is good.

Marriage and Culture

God, all through Scripture, explains what is the rightful way for a marriage to operate. That's what we're going to be looking at here. Why? Because there's a natural conflict built into the marriage. If you entered a marriage relationship—and many young couples do—you may have thought, 'All of this is going to bring fulfillment to my life.' It's going to bring satisfaction.

I've had people come to marriage counseling. I've asked, "What is the problem?" They said, "I'm just not satisfied." I said, "Well, marriage is not designed to satisfy you." Sometimes they'll say, "I just don't feel love." Marriage is not for love. Your love and your personal worth or dignity come from God. You will not find it in an imperfect, fallen person who is preloaded to rule over you or try to control you. What kind of craziness is that?

We tend to believe this person we love is going to be the fulfillment of our life. But this person may be your worst nightmare. They may fulfill their sinful tendencies, and you may fulfill your sinful tendencies. You will have constant conflict in that relationship. However, the beautiful thing about it is that God provides us with a prescription on how to resolve that. And it is perfect. God has taken a man and a woman who are trying to manage each other. He is putting them together as a unified front and teaching them to manage what they're supposed to manage. That's what a Christian marriage will do.

And a mother and a father together united will manage their children and everything that comes into their part of the garden that they have to tend. That is God's purpose. But if you notice, God says, He made them; male and female He created them.

Unfortunately, this is not true according to our society. Not only is this relationship inbuilt with conflict between a male and a female, but culture and society come in and try to wreck marriage even further.

So, God's establishment of the family is to create order in society. It's meant to create structure. It's a man and a woman together as one united front to manage what God has put before us. But sin has wrecked that. So when a man and woman have children, and they're spending all their time managing each other, they don't manage their children, and they don't manage the things that God wants them to manage.

And then you have society swoop in on it. And society starts trying to erase the lines that God established. If you'll notice, God is very clear on this--that a marriage is between a man and a woman.

Recall Genesis 1:27, *So God created man in His own image; in the image of God He created him; male and female He created them.*

There are only two genders—male and female. This is from a Christian worldview, of course. Unbelievers can believe anything they want to, and I don't care. But for a Christian, there is male and female. That's it. That's all there is because that is what God created.

Society says plenty of other stuff, and it creates confusion for people. For example, one of the things society promotes and pushes is homosexuality. Homosexuality is very common in our society. I told my Sunday School class this morning that I don't watch TV much. I watched some sports in the fall when football was on, and I'll watch a show where a guy drives around and rates local hole-in-the-wall restaurants. But I don't watch the news or any of the standard nonsense.

What amazes me is when I turn the TV on, and I watch a Texas A&M football game, I'll watch that game, and if I didn't know any better, the commercials that come on would lead me to believe that 50% of the people in America are homosexual. In reality, they make up less than two percent, but see, it's an agenda being pushed on you. And people come to the point where they accept it, because if you don't, you become an outcast and get pushed aside.

I have friends who are homosexual. How do I treat those people? I don't treat them differently than I would any other friend. Their relationship is their business. My chief concern isn't the relationship between homosexuals. My chief concern is what is being pushed on society.

What about transgenderism? Where should we stand now? Transgenderism is a mental illness. When asked for the definition of a woman, a recent nominee for the Supreme Court, Ms. Brown, was unable to define what a woman was. As a pastor and a human being, I can define what a woman is. I can define what a man is. And I'm not a biologist. There is a man, and there is a woman. I know what a dog is as well. There's a male dog. There's a female dog. It's pretty obvious. I can neuter that male dog, but it is still a male dog. It doesn't change a bit. There's no in between on dogs, there's no in between on chickens, there's no in between on horses.

There's no in between on humans. It's a male or a female.

But I continue to see how often the Church in our society is terrified of stating what is true. Stop being afraid of speaking the truth. If we don't start standing up for what's right or pointing out what's wrong, we're going to lose the entire society.

Standing Up for Biblical Marriage

God is the one who gave us the authority to have dominion over creation. And we are stepping back and surrendering that, letting the fringe element rise up and dictate norms. If everyone just goes along like a bunch of little sheep, we continue to hear, Okay, I don't really see anything wrong with it. I don't want to be judgmental.

What are you afraid of? Stop being afraid of people. People can kill you. People can destroy you. They can grind you to a pulp. But God says, I can throw your soul into eternal separation. You better learn who to fear. He tells us to stop the fear of men. Fear of man brings the snare. The snare is when man becomes afraid to speak up for right or wrong.

We are losing our culture, and we're losing society, and we're losing it in the arena of the family—simply because we're stepping back and letting the fringe element take over. It's time for Christians to wake up in this country and realize we have a moral responsibility given to us by God to take dominion over the creation and to be a witness. We are to be salt and light to the world around us.

People need to know what the truth is. And if we're silent because we're afraid, then we're part of the problem. That's all there is to it. Where else are they going to hear the truth? God has put us in the position to speak the truth in love. We don't do it in a mean, condemning, or cruel way—but we speak the truth.

The truth will always win. Truth will get someone on the right track. Truth will move people from sin to righteousness. But if we don't take a stand, and if we don't support people who take a stand for what's right, we're going to lose this society. Your children are going to suffer. Your grandchildren are going to suffer. And the generations after them are going to suffer even more. There is an attack on the family and anything that stands for right and wrong in our society. However, we're on the winning team. If we stand for the truth, then God will come alongside us when the trouble comes. We must start believing our Bibles and believe in God. Stand against sin in a loving and caring way, but we have to stand for the truth.

Notice what all of these assaults are coming against. They're coming against the family. What happens when the family breaks down? Order and structure and society begin to break down. If our children aren't seeing a unified front between mom and dad, they're going to look elsewhere. Why? They are geared to look for that. That's just the way man is made. We seek out unity.

We are created in the likeness of God, and the only way we can find our true purpose and direction in life is when we are rightly aligned with God. That's the only way fulfillment comes. God's design for the family is 1+1=1. A united, strong, fortified front that takes dominion and manages everything around it.

The breakdown of the family goes back to the garden and the lack of unity between a husband and a wife. In Chapter 2, we'll take a look at Colossians, where we are shown what comes next and how we can fix what has been broken.

CHAPTER 2
Roles
The Role of a Husband and Wife

Wives, submit to your own husbands, as is fitting in the Lord. Husbands, love your wives and do not be bitter toward them. Children, obey your parents in all things, for this is well pleasing to the Lord. Fathers, do not provoke your children, lest they become discouraged.—Colossians 3:18–21

The apostle Paul now speaks directly to the family dynamic in Colossians 3:18–21, offering a framework for how husbands, wives, and children should relate to one another. These verses offer timeless guidance on how to restore and strengthen family relationships, especially in the context of a fallen world where sin has brought brokenness and division. Paul's words are not merely cultural instructions, but gospel-centered directives that reveal how Christ can redeem and renew what has been fractured by sin.

This passage calls for a radical shift in the way spouses and parents interact, promoting humility, love, and mutual respect. Paul paints a vision of the Christian family as a place of healing, where the gospel shapes every relationship, mending the effects of sin and fostering unity, love, and peace.

"Wives, submit to your own husbands, as is fitting in the Lord" Colossians 3:18. For some, this verse can have a very negative connotation, particularly if you don't understand the background and what Paul is actually saying in the passage, as well as how it relates to the whole of the Christian faith.

The passage continues to say in verse 19, "Husbands love your wives and do not be bitter toward them." That has a whole different idea when you understand what the problem in the relationship is. This section is part of a bigger whole, and the bigger whole is for us to put on the new man and take off the old man. It's addressing basic Christian relationships and how we as believers should live our lives and practice our faith within that family unit.

We have to remember this section in relation to the passage in Genesis we looked at in the first chapter. Man had basically two assignments before him. One was to tend and keep the garden and to have dominion over all the creation—so man was put in a position of authority to have dominion over the earth. The second thing was to walk with God and to bring glory to God, but sin damaged that.

"Adam said, 'This is now bone of my bone and flesh of my flesh, she shall be called woman because she was taken out of man.'"
—Genesis 2:23

Adam is declaring that Eve is a part of him, that she's his complement. She is his fulfillment, and God put them together to make a team. "Therefore, man will leave his father and mother and be joined to his wife." The word join, here, means to stick like glue—they're to adhere to one another.

"And they became one flesh." In time, that sticky-like-glue becomes tighter and tighter. That's how God designed it. And from here, we read that they were both naked, and they were not ashamed. Everything is functioning well and as it should. Then, as we've already discussed, sin comes along. The serpent came into the garden, they ate the fruit, and man failed, after which God put a curse on the marriage relationship.

Through the course of God addressing the curse, He says to Eve, Your desire will be for your husband, and he will rule over you (*Genesis 3:16*). That is the curse right there. So you have a husband and wife who are one unified force, sin separates that, and then within the marriage relationship, the woman's desire is to control the man, and the man's desire is to control the woman.

So what is the root problem in a marriage relationship? It's twofold. First, man is a sinful being. Because of sin, it is difficult for mankind to get along without being in a relationship, just living life. It's tough to get along with people all right. But when you get two sinful people and put them in a home together, there's going to be some conflict just from the simple aspect of mankind's nature.

What we're going to look at in Colossians 18 is how to get rid of this part where the man is trying to rule the woman the woman is trying to rule the man. That's what it is all about, and this passage aims to straighten that out.

First Things First

The first step in straightening out this relationship conflict is to deal with the sinfulness of man. Even if we're not in a relationship, there's conflict. But when two people move in together, there's going to be even more conflict. There's a constant back and forth in that relationship, constantly going at each other, constantly putting the pressure on the other one—and then, when that happens, the other one puts that pressure back. You push me, I'll push you.

Sin has destroyed everything that God created, so how do we straighten this out?

God told Nicodemus that the way to fix this is to be born again. You have to be born from above. What does it mean for a person to be born again or born from above?

What it means is that when man sinned in the garden, God said the day Adam and Eve ate the fruit, they would surely die. So, man died in that garden, but we think of a physical death when we hear the word die.

But the word die used there is that man died spiritually, and as a result of spiritual death, he will experience eternal death. The way God remedied that is with the new birth. When we talk about man being spiritually dead, it does not mean that man ceases to have spiritual desire. It just means that instead of rightly relating to God, they will seek other idols. The only way you're going to relate to Creator God is to have an active spirit in relationship to God.

If your spirit is dead, God has to bring your spirit alive, and then His Spirit comes to live within you. That's what the new birth is all about—being born again means that your spirit is brought alive.

But let's consider physical death. Physical death means that your body has been separated from the physical world in the sense of being able to respond to it. When a person dies, or they code out in the hospital, doctors will go through various tests to determine if that person is alive. They have all the machines that can pick up brain waves and heartbeat, but what they're looking for is signs of physical life.

If you poke a dead person, they don't respond to physical stimuli.

They're dead to the physical world. It doesn't mean they cease to exist; that body is right there, it just means it doesn't respond to the physical world. So, when a man is spiritually dead, he does not respond to the true and living God because the only way to respond to the true and living God is when our spirit is alive, because it is with our spirit that we worship God.

When God created man, He created him both physically with a body, and He created an immaterial side of man, which is the spirit and the soul. Spirit and soul, you can't see. Soul is your personality, your desires, your likes, your dislikes, things that make you, you. Your spirit is how you relate to God. Now, a person who is outside of Jesus Christ has a spirit, but he cannot relate to the living God because the Spirit must be made alive.

If you talk to people who are not born again, they don't have a relationship with God, and they will often tell you, "I'm a spiritual person." We're hearing that more and more in our culture. Why? Because we're created in the image and likeness of God, and there's an inward spirit in us that yearns to have a relationship with the Spirit of God.

I was out at a prison once, and they were having a pagan feast. A chaplain has to cover all the religious spaces, and on this particular day, I was talking to the chaplain and this group. One of those guys in the back said they were having a pagan feast. I asked who was in the room where the festival was being held. He told me it was Satanists and others, different groups that are classified as pagan. I told him I'd never been to a pagan feast, and I'd like to go in there. He told me to help myself. I went in there and introduced myself to them.

I said, "What y'all all doing?" They said, "We are having a pagan feast. Would you like to join?" I said, "Sure, I'm in."

I got to talking to these men and every one of them said, "I'm a very spiritual person, but I have nothing to do with Jesus Christ." As a matter of fact, they said they didn't like Jesus Christ to varying degrees.

Some of them were more defiant than others, but they all said, "I'm a spiritual person." Man is a spiritual being, but to rightly relate to God, our human spirit has to be brought alive to God, and that is called the new birth.

God brings your spirit alive. He not only brings your spirit alive; His Spirit comes to live within you, and it is only then that you can worship God.

John 4:24 tells us that God is spirit and those who worship Him must worship Him in spirit and truth. So, we've got to have a spirit, and we've got to have the truth. Worship is prescriptive. God tells us how to worship Him. He tells us what is. We don't make up our own way. There are many people who say they worship God in their own way, and I always want them to explain that to me.

"Well, you know I don't believe you have to be in church, I don't believe you have to do this or that," they usually say.

And I say, "Well, there are certain things that, according to Scripture, you have to have that are in line with what God wants and desires." When you're the omnipotent, omniscient being, and you created everything that is in the physical world, then you're in a position to tell that physical world how they're going to worship you. I'm just trying to break it down and make it simple.

God describes to us how to worship Him, but to worship Him, you must have the Spirit. The Spirit within you produces fruit, and one of the fruits of the Spirit is love. Christ, when He was here on earth, described this relationship that believers have. He said this is a relationship whereby you love one another.

Then Comes Love

John 13:34 shows the beginning of the Upper Room discourse, when Christ was meeting with His disciples right before His crucifixion. Verse 34 says, *A new commandment I give to you, that you love one another; as I have loved you, that you also love one another. By this, all will know that you're my disciples if you have love for one another.*

When a person is born again, they are to love one another. We are to love our brothers and sisters, and we're to love God. These are the two relationships: to love God with all your heart, mind, and soul, and to love your neighbors as yourself. The love that God talks about is the love that He produces. The agape love that is used in this verse is an act of the will. It's when we choose to love people unconditionally.

Agape love isn't the sort of love that has feelings or emotion—that is filial love, or brotherly love. This word, this agape love, is also used for your enemies. Love your enemy. We are not going to have good feelings toward our enemies, because if we did, they wouldn't be our enemies. No, when He talks about love here, it is an act of the will. So, how is that love expressed?

We begin by treating others with common decency and common courtesy. If my enemy is thirsty, I give him something to drink; if he's hungry, I give him something to eat. I don't act rude or vengeful. I'm just kind and courteous, but I don't have warm feelings toward them. In our relationships, we can have agape love for another person, and we can also have filial love. Filial love will determine the depth of that relationship.

You likely also have friends that are real friends—I'm talking about real friends before Facebook came along. We have friends at different levels.

It was the same for Jesus Christ. He had Peter, James, and John in

His inner circle. Those were His dear friends. Then, He had the disciples, then He had the 70, then He had the multitude, and then He had the world. These relationships have different levels of trust relating to filial love.

Agape love is saying, "I love you because you're a human being. I love you because I'm choosing to love you." When He says in these verses, "Love one another," He is talking about believers loving their brother or sister in Christ.

> *Owe no one anything except to love one another, for he who loves another has fulfilled the law.*—Romans 13:8

Love is a necessary component of a person who is born again. In a Christian relationship, you are in a relationship if your wife is a believer or if your husband is a believer. You're primarily in a Christian relationship, and you have a commandment from God to love your brother and sister in Christ.

One of the very fundamental levels of love in my relationship with my wife is that she is also my sister in Christ. I am her brother in Christ, and so I have a responsibility to exercise basic Christian love toward my wife, and she does toward me. In this idea of "husbands love your wives as Christ loved the Church," He is talking about a whole different level of love that takes place, because there should already be love there.

If you're not married and you're looking for someone, don't compromise. When a woman chooses a man or a man chooses a woman, they need a partner who is going to move them up in their walk with God, not move them down.

Oftentimes, young girls will marry a guy who is spiritually dead in the water. When asked how his relationship with the Lord is, she will often reply that they never really talk about that much. That's a major red light warning sign, because he will get worse once you marry. He's not going to get better. The best you will see from a man is while you're dating.

If he is a Christian man, in time, he will grow in that relationship, and he'll eventually start doing the things that he did when he dated you, but it takes time. The same goes for guys looking for a wife. Don't marry a woman if you have to go down a notch to get married. I have worked in premarital counseling, and I've seen it numerous times.

There was one couple who sticks in my mind, vividly, from around twenty years ago. I told them to come in for premarital counseling, and they said they would. The guy showed up, and there was no girl there.

I said, "Your fiancé is late."

He replied, "Well, she's not into the church thing."

I said, "This is going to be a whole different counseling session, and I'm going to advise you on some stuff that you might want to heed." I warned him, "You're headed for a train wreck unless she gets saved. Is she a believer?"

"Well, you know, I think she loves God. I think she's spiritual," he replied.

"The devil is spiritual, so it doesn't really mean a whole lot. Do you think she loves God? When he said yes, I asked, "What makes you think she loves God?"

As we continued in this conversation, it became clear his fiancée had no relationship with God at all.

I asked, "Why would you want to marry a woman like that? Why would you do that? It doesn't make sense. You can't be equally yoked together. You'll have enough problems as it is in marriage. Don't have more problems—be discerning."

You choose who you're going to marry, and that choice is for life. There are people who will spend more time picking out a car and are more discerning about a car than they are a partner for life.

If you went to a car dealership and the guy was selling you a used car and he said, "This is an 8-cylinder, but it's only six of them work," you wouldn't just shrug it off. You wouldn't say, "I can deal with that. And you know, maybe we can get the AC fixed later on or something." You're not going to pay top dollar for that. You would ask to look at another model.

But there are some guys who meet a girl who doesn't love the Lord, and he just thinks, "You know, we can fix that later." They don't care anything about church, and they don't care anything about reading scriptures. It's not that they might not come to love the Lord someday, but that's a pretty big risk to take when you are talking about the rest of your life.

When you come into a marriage relationship with a man and a woman who are brothers and sisters in Christ, so there's a fundamental bottom line, and it's rooted in Christ.

Submission and Peace

> *And do not be drunk with wine, in which is dissipation; but be filled with the Spirit, speaking to one another in psalms and hymns and spiritual songs, singing and making melody in your heart to the Lord, giving thanks always for all things to God the Father in the name of our Lord Jesus Christ, submitting to one another in the fear of God.*—Ephesians 5:18–21

This is a contrast. When a person is filled—the Greek word for this means to control or to saturate—with wine, what happens? It affects the way they live. It affects the way they talk; it affects the way they walk.

When we reach verse 21, there's that old evil word submitting.

Again, we remember, this is in the relationship of a brother and sister to Christ. Then, we look at the next verse.

Wives, submit to your own husbands, as to the Lord.—Ephesians 5:22

Why would He have submission in the verses before and then submission again? Because submission is a common part of a Christian relationship, a normative part of a Christian relationship.

What does it mean when I submit to my brother in Christ? It means I'm willing to defer to them, and they're willing to defer to me. There are no issues; we don't make mountains out of molehills. You learn to let things go and to mutually exist together. That's submitting. It means you respect each other.

But above all these things, put on love, which is the bond of perfection, and let the peace of God rule in your hearts.—Colossians 3:14–15a

Remember, the peace of God is a guide to your life and lets you know if things are right. It's to let you know if things are going the way they should go. If you don't have the peace of God, it is telling you there's something wrong in a relationship.

No matter what relationship we are talking about, when you worry, you're taking God from His rightful place, and you're saying, "I need to handle these issues, God." That is sinful. And when you have sin in your life, you're not going to have the peace of God.

The peace of God is basically the umpire. It lets you know if something is out of bounds.

And let the peace of God rule in your hearts, to which also you were called in one body; and be thankful. Let the Word of Christ

dwell in you richly in all wisdom, teaching and admonishing one another in psalms and hymns and spiritual songs, singing with grace in your hearts to the Lord. And whatever you do in word or deed, do all in the name of the Lord Jesus, giving thanks to God the Father through Him.—Colossians 3:15–17

Verse 16 of this passage is the same as the spirit being controlled by the spirit in Ephesians 5. The Word of Christ dwelling in you richly is going to produce the same thing as being filled with the Spirit. They are synonymous.

We are urged, *whatever we do in word or deed, do all in the name of the Lord Jesus Christ* (Colossians 3:17). It means we don't do anything in the Christian life except for what God approves. That's why we submit one to another. We have a compatible relationship. Both of these verses provide instructions that are specific to the family because they address the roles in the family.

This first part is dealing with sin that has separated us one from another. The second part is going to deal with the specific roles that relate to the idea of the man wanting to control the woman and the woman wanting to control the man. We're seeing that submission is not just the woman—submission is first, each of your relationships with God as born-again believers. Then it's in your specific roles as husbands and wives.

Instead of woman trying to control the man, what is the woman going to do? She respects the man. And instead of the man trying to control the woman, he loves the woman. Marriage then becomes a relationship of ministry, whereby the wife ministers to the husband, and the husband ministers to the wife. Why? So they can be one unified team. That's the way God has designed it. The first way to get that team going is to deal with sin, and the second way to get it going is to deal with these relationships where you become a team.

If the family goes, so goes a nation, and so goes everything else. It is a basic, fundamental example of what respect and oneness is supposed to look like. As parents, our responsibility is to model what a Christian man is and what a Christian woman is in a relationship.

And yes, there's still going to be conflict. But what do they do when they have that conflict in that relationship? One of them will go and apologize to the other, and then the other one apologizes, and they work everything out.

What are you teaching? You're teaching children forgiveness.

The fundamental step is basic Christian love in a relationship. That is spiritually yielding over self, because the essence of sin is 'self.' If you want to know what sin is, watch a toddler. They display self extremely well. What you have is mine, what I have is mine, and if you have something I want, I'll take it, and if I don't get it, I'll cry about it. That's all sin is.

Sin is not wanting to do what God wants but doing what we want to do. Sin is when we don't care what others think because we've got our rights. Sin is not yielding.

Salvation is spiritually yielding over self, service over self, others before self. It's putting self under and making others better.

Society and the Family

In a marriage relationship, a husband and a wife should seek to help each other to serve each other. That is a fundamental building block in a marriage relationship. Basic Christian duty submits.

It's important to remember this as the families in our nation go into more turmoil and start reverberating outside of that building block.

By moving outside of that fundamental building block, by moving outside of submission, we destroy what God intended to be a unified front. It becomes disintegrated, blown to pieces.

As we looked at in chapter one, the family is constantly under assault and attack. Why? Because if you can destroy the family, you can destroy an entire society.

What comes to mind when we consider changes in our society over the last 50 years? One of the first things that popped up around that time was pornography.

The big author of pornography was Hugh Hefner, and he started this open love nonsense. He made pornography readily available. How is pornography dangerous to a family? How is pornography dangerous to your life?

Because it depicts women in a dehumanizing way. It depicts women in a way God never intended women to be depicted. When God created the woman, He knew what He was doing.

Men are physically stimulated—it doesn't take much, but pornography takes women and puts them in a dehumanizing way. How did culture embrace Hugh Hefner? At first, there was some pushback, but over time he became very acceptable, very honored, and very admired—so much so that they gave them TV programs.

After the early days of Hugh Hefner influencing society, we started seeing how feminism came onto the scene. What was feminism? The early feminists began back in the late 50s. Groups of women started devaluing men. To a certain extent, I can't blame them because a lot of men had treated women unjustly. Women have been oppressed since the Garden of Eden. They've been held down, and they don't get equal opportunity. They have been excluded, didn't get promotions, didn't get paid, etc. I can understand their frustration.

But what happened was, they used that anger, and they fed that anger, and they began to dehumanize the male and the family and enjoyed making men look useless and worthless. Whereas, if men worked the way God intended them to in a marriage relationship, women would want to elevate man because that man is there to help that woman and move her up in the world.

But it continued from there. We saw the ERA, the Equal Rights Amendment, which was a big thing back in the 70s. It was a declaration for women to take control, to dominate.

And then it progresses on from there, and you started seeing the homosexual movement, and then now we're living in the transgender movement. These are all perversions of what God intended. I have no doubt that it is going to move into the pedophilia movement, and then it is going to go to bestiality.

Romans 1 makes it clear, and we see what happens when people destroy God's order and design. It's a downward progression. How do you stop that? You stop that by making strong marriages and building people who honor the relationship of marriage and stand strong for it. I'll be the first to tell you, I don't care what the lost world out there does, but when the Church starts embracing what the lost world does, then the Church is in trouble, folks.

The Church is in trouble.

I don't care what kind of relationship a person is in; I can love that person, and I can be kind and nice to that person. The Church is not called to beat these people down or to run them into the ground. The Church is called to love them. And the most loving thing we can do is give the light of Jesus Christ and life to them and guide them to be in their original position that God intended for them. But you can't condone, and you can't go along to get along.

You've got to stand firmly for what God has made you to be. You've got to use the Bible as your guide, and one of the fundamental principles of the Bible is to love one another. Love others as you'd want them to love you, but that does not mean that you have to accept what they do. I don't love people because I accept everything they do. I love my children. My children would do some crazy stuff when they were younger, but it didn't change my love for them. It might break my heart, and it might make me sad, and at times, I might allow their behavior to get me angry.

Notice I said allow me to get angry, because they can't make me angry. Anger is a choice that you make. I'll allow their behavior to get me angry at times, but the love I have for them never changes. You can go to the end of the earth for one of your children when you truly love them. And if you truly love people, you will treat them as people regardless of what they love.

But in the marriage relationship, God says we need a unified front, and that comes through Jesus Christ. Here's what I mean. You see, that first Adam messed the whole thing up, and so God sent the last Adam, Jesus Christ.

The first Adam, in the garden, blew the whole game. Then the last Adam, Jesus Christ, comes. He's 100% God, He is 100% man, both in one person. He came to redeem the creation back to God. When He came here on earth, He lived as a Jewish male under the law, and lived the law perfectly, and went to the cross. When He went to the cross, with one hand He could connect with man, and with the other hand He could connect to God. He is the bridge between God and man.

He died on the cross when God put the sin of mankind on Him. What was that sin? It was the imputed sin of Adam. It was the inherited sin of Adam, and it is all of our personal sin. The imputed sin of Adam says that if I had been in the garden, I would have eaten the fruit too.

People say Adam blew it for all of us. You would have blown it too because God imputes the sin of Adam and you. It's just as if you were in the garden, as if I were in the garden. But when Jesus Christ died, He died for the imputed sin, the inherited sin, and all my personal sin.

He bore that sin on His body, was buried, and on the third day He rose again, because God accepted payment for that sin. And now, that sin barrier is gone, and I can have that relationship with Him because of what the last Adam did. Now that I have that relationship, my spirit is brought alive. God's spirit is living within me, and I love the Lord God with my heart, mind, and soul. I love my neighbors as myself, and my partner in marriage is my sister in Christ.

Because of this, I have an obligation to treat her as such, and she has an obligation to treat me the same. We submit one to another. Before we get into role relationships, there's already a mutual submission in there. What the role relationships are going to do is show you how to reverse this back-and-forth nonsense in a relationship, to come back to a unified force.

God designed marriage with a perfect plan. We deal with the sin first, then we deal with the roles, and we practice that day by day by day. We do it as a unified front, moving forward, because that is the hope. The hope is that God can change the world. It's never too late. God can change the world, but before we want to see God work in the world, He is going to work in His own home. He is going to work with His own people. Christians have to get marriage relationships right because we are to demonstrate what God's perfect plan is. Understand that marriage is also a picture of Christ and the Church. Unity, oneness, and togetherness are all Bible-based. We are a united front, facing the world to bring glory to God.

CHAPTER 3
The Submission of Christ
Christ and the Church

In this chapter, we're going to look at the submission of Christ. We'll consider how Christ did two things. First, how He submitted to the Father. Second, how He submitted to man. Part of the reason we need to see this in light of Scripture is to set the stage for what submission truly is. Unfortunately, it is a subject that has been taken out of context to a great degree.

As I mentioned in the last chapter, submission has gotten a negative connotation in many churches. What does submission really mean? It is not the man's responsibility to make the wife submit; rather, the wife submits to the will of the father. We are going to look at that and what that actually entails before we get into the individual roles in the family.

Let's first consider the headship of Christ. We have to look at His position because He is referred to as the head. The husband is also referred to as the head, so we need to know what it means to have headship.

How does Christ have headship?

He is the image of the invisible God, the firstborn over all creation.—Colossians 1:15

When it says that He is the image, it means He is the exact physical representation of the invisible God. When Christ took on human flesh, He lived out life here on earth and did His ministry here on earth to show us what the Father is like. If you want to know what God is like, read the Gospels. They tell us about Jesus Christ, and that is how God is.

For by Him all things were created that are in heaven and that are on earth, visible and invisible, whether thrones or dominions or principalities or powers. All things were created through Him and for Him. And He is before all things, and in Him all things consist. And He is the head of the body, the Church, who is the beginning, the firstborn from the dead, that in all things He may have the preeminence.—Colossians 1:16–18

That's total headship seen in Scripture. It is as high as you can get, as far as headship goes. Not only does He have a headship as creator, but He also has headship as sustainer. Verse 17 tells us, *He is before all things and in Him all things consist.* He holds everything together; He sustains the universe.

The universe doesn't run on its own; it runs by the control of God. God orchestrates it. There are a bunch of natural processes that are in place, but God ensures those processes stay where they are and that they function properly. Not only did He create, but He also controls the creation. This verse tells us He is the head of the body. What is the body?

The Church is the body. He is the creator; He is the sustainer of all the creation, and then you go within that, and it tells us He is the head of the Church, the body of Christ. Who is the beginning? The firstborn, born from the dead, that in all things He may have preeminence. Being the firstborn from the dead means that He ranks first and foremost over all that exists.

It's not talking about birth order; it is talking about preeminence. That word has a purpose clause and tells you why or what the first part of that sentence means. It means that in everything, Christ ranks supreme overall.

> *And He put all things under His feet, and gave Him to be head over all things to the Church.*—Ephesians 1:22

The Church is His body, the fullness of Him, so He has headship over the Church.

> *. . . that we should no longer be children, tossed to and fro and carried about with every wind of doctrine, by the trickery of men, in the cunning craftiness of deceitful plotting, but, speaking the truth in love, may grow up in all things into Him who is the head—Christ.*—Ephesians 4:14-15

Christ is the head, having headship and preeminence over all that exists. Not just the creation, but the Church too, so Christ is overall, and that tells us about His position.

The Plan of God

The second thing is this: Christ submitted to the Father. Submission is not a bad thing. It's made to be that way. Submission is a part of the natural order that God has established in His perfect plan.

> *Jesus said to them, 'My food is to do the will of Him who sent Me, and to finish His work.'*—John 4:34

It's quite clear in this passage that Christ is submitting to the Father. He is doing the Father's will. When Christ came here to earth, He took on a human body to execute the plan of God.

What was the plan of God? The plan of God was to redeem mankind back to the Father. And so Christ did that, but in order to do it, He had to submit to the Father.

> *I can of Myself do nothing. As I hear, I judge; and My judgment is righteous, because I do not seek My own will but the will of the Father who sent Me.*—John 5:30

What Christ is saying is that He is bringing Himself under the Father to carry out the plan of the Father.

The Godhead is made up of God the Father, God the Son, and God the Holy Spirit—coequal, all possessing the same deity in one person. Now, trying to explain the Trinity is beyond the scope of this book. I had a course in seminary called Trinitarianism, and we spent an entire semester dealing with this subject. So, we won't attempt it in one chapter of this book.

However, at the conclusion of the subject, you will come up with one conclusion: the Trinity is a concept that is outside of human understanding and comprehension completely. It's part of the mystery of God. You could illustrate the Trinity in a lot of ways. A lot of people say it's like water—you've got water as a liquid, water as a solid (ice), and water as a vapor.

I've heard the illustration of an egg. You've got the eggshell, the egg white, and the egg yolk, all three in one. Trees, you've got the roots, the trunk, and the branches. You could come up with all these illustrations, but every illustration will ultimately break down because you're dealing with the subject of God. What you end up doing with these examples is committing one of the common heresies in the early church. These illustrations give Christ and the Father and the Spirit different modes, and it is just one God, but He is doing different things—that's where it all breaks down.

We have to step back from it and understand that when we get to heaven, in the presence of God, we will understand completely. But we have to accept by faith that there is Father, Son, and the Holy Spirit. They have the same deity in one person, outside of human understanding. You cannot put your mind around that unless you're a special creature. You've got to accept it by faith because that is the way the Scripture presents it.

In God's plan, the Son submitted to the Father to execute the plan of God. He was never less than the Father; He never was less than the Holy Spirit, yet He submitted. So, He does not lose His individuality; He does not lose His personhood; he does not lose His deity. He simply carries out the plan of God.

> *For I have come down from heaven, not to do My own will, but the will of Him who sent Me. This is the will of the Father who sent Me, that of all He has given Me I should lose nothing but should raise it up at the last day. And this is the will of Him who sent Me, that everyone who sees the Son and believes in Him may have everlasting life; and I will raise Him up at the last day.*—John 6:38–40

Yet again, you see where He is submitting to the will of the Father. We see this again a little further on.

> *Then Jesus said to them, 'When you lift up the Son of Man, then you will know that I am He, and that I do nothing of Myself; but as My Father taught Me, I speak these things. And He who sent Me is with Me. The Father has not left Me alone, for I always do those things that please Him.'*—John 8:28–29

There's submission within the Godhead, so Christ submits to the Father to carry out the Father's will. He executes the will of the Father. The incarnation was the submission. Christ takes on a human body, and He limits Himself and lives here on earth to bring God to us, to explain God to us, to show us what God is like very clearly in Scripture.

> *Let nothing be done through selfish ambition or conceit, but in lowliness of mind let each esteem others better than himself. Let each of you look out not only for his own interests, but also for the interests of others. Let this mind be in you which was also in Christ Jesus, who, being in the form of God, did not consider it robbery to be equal with God, but made Himself of no reputation, taking the form of a bondservant, and coming in the likeness of men.—* Philippians 2:3–7

There's that mutual submission between believers. I'm to lift you up, you're to lift me up. What does that do? It keeps conflict out.

A Christian's perspective is that the husband lifts up the wife, the wife lifts up the husband—there's a mutual working between the two. The word form in Philippians 2:6 means more faith; it means that He is God. It doesn't mean He was less; the word more faith means an exact representation.

The word robbery is a very poor translation, because of how we use that word today. Your Bible may have a different translation. The word robbery as used in the text means something to hang on to. In other words, I am fully God, but I'm willing to let that go and submit to the Father. Or to say, Me and the Father are equal, but to carry out the Father's plan, I'm going to let that go, I'm going to release that.

And then He says that He made Himself of no reputation. It means that He voluntarily chose not to exercise some of His divine attributes.

It is what we refer to as the cyanosis passage because the word that is used there is the word cyanosis, and it simply means that Christ chose not to use some of His attributes.

What did He do? Christ came to earth, incarnated God as the last Adam, to undo what the first Adam did. The first Adam came into the garden, and God gave him dominion over everything. What did He do? He submitted Himself to the serpent. The last Adam comes, Jesus Christ, God, with a human body. He comes to the same earth, and what does He do? He is tempted in a wilderness by that same old devil, but He rejects the devil and submits Himself to God. I did not come to do my will, but the will of the one who sent me. So, He comes in perfect submission to God to redeem the creation back to the Father. He had to take on the human body to do that.

He had to live as a human being here on earth without sin, an undiminished deity in one person. The only begotten of the Father, the unique God man, and that is what he did. He lived here on earth as the God-man. He made Himself of no reputation, taking on the form of a servant and coming in the likeness of men.

He has a human body, but He has no sin. We see it in Scripture that He, Himself, became obedient to the point of death on a cross—the most shameful death someone could suffer. God has highly exalted Him, giving the name which is above every name, that at the name of Jesus, every knee should bow. Those in heaven, on the earth, and under the earth—every tongue should confess that Jesus is Lord to the glory of the Father.

The Submission of Christ

Jesus voluntarily submits Himself to the Father, and He voluntarily carries out the Father's plan. You have the headship of Christ, you have the submission to the Father, and you have Christ, who not only sub-mitted Himself to the Father, but Christ committed Himself to man. That's as low as you can get.

Therefore, submit yourselves to every ordinance of man for the Lord's sake, whether to the king as supreme, or to governors, as to those who are sent by him for the punishment of evildoers and for the praise of those who do good. For this is the will of God, that by doing good you may put to silence the ignorance of foolish men—as free, yet not using liberty as a cloak for vice, but as bondservants of God. Honor all people. Love the brotherhood. Fear God. Honor the king.—1 Peter 2:13-17

Servants, be submissive to your masters with all fear, not only to the good and gentle, but also to the harsh. For this is commendable, if because of conscience toward God one endures grief, suffering wrongfully. For what credit is it if, when you are beaten for your faults, you take it patiently? But when you do good and suffer, if you take it patiently, this is commendable before God. For to this you were called, because Christ also suffered for us, leaving us an example, that you should follow His steps:—1 Peter 2:18-21

Who committed no sin, nor was deceit found in His mouth; — 1 Peter 4:2

Who, when He was reviled, did not revile in return; when He suffered, He did not threaten, but committed Himself to Him who judges righteously; who Himself bore our sins in His own body on the tree, that we, having died to sins, might live for righteous-ness—by whose stripes you were healed. For you were like sheep going astray, but have now returned to the Shepherd and Overseer of your souls.—1 Peter 2:23–25

We see submission in this passage. He is fully submitted to the Father, even though He is submitting Himself to man. When people took advantage of Christ, we realize that what power He had, He submitted as man, or they could have never crucified Christ—they couldn't lay a hand on Him.

Wives, likewise, be submissive to your own husbands, that even if some do not obey the word, they, without a word, may be won by the conduct of their wives, when they observe your chaste conduct accompanied by fear. Do not let your adornment be merely outward—arranging the hair, wearing gold, or putting on fine apparel—rather let it be the hidden person of the heart, with the incorruptible beauty of a gentle and quiet spirit, which is very precious in the sight of God. For in this manner, in former times, the holy women who trusted in God also adorned themselves, being submissive to their own husbands, as Sarah obeyed Abraham, calling him lord, whose daughters you are if you do good and are not afraid with any terror.—1 Peter 3:1-6

Husbands, likewise, dwell with them with understanding, giving honor to the wife, as to the weaker vessel, and as being heirs together of the grace of life, that your prayers may not be hindered.—1 Peter 3:7

Finally, all of you be of one mind, having compassion for one another; love as brothers, be tenderhearted, be courteous; not returning evil for evil or reviling for reviling, but on the contrary blessing, knowing that you were called to this, that you may inherit a blessing.—1 Peter 3:8-9

What is He saying there? The greatest beauty you can have is your character. The outside appearance is fine, but the innocence that matters needs to be on the inside. That's what's important. What kind of a person are you on the inside?

You see how this whole passage, everything in here, is designed for unity? That is the purpose and the reason behind it. Christ submits to the Father, and Christ submits Himself to man. Now, let's look specifically at His submission to man.

Looking back at 1 Peter 2:21, you notice through this whole passage that there's this submission that is going on, and He concludes it in 1 Peter 3:8, with a call to compassion toward one another.

That is the underlying relationship in a marriage. A husband and wife are courteous and tender-hearted to each other. They treat each other as brother and sister in Christ. That's the first thing that takes place. They treat each other in a kind manner. Christian relationships, marriage, is designed for the man and the wife to mutually support one another. That's the way the relationship is designed. That's the way the relationship was in the garden before sin, and that is the way God wants the relationship now.

The first step in marriage counseling, if you're having trouble in marriage, is to draw closer to God. Draw closer to God, because you're to submit one to another in the body of Christ as believers. We may disagree on something, but we decide that the unity of the body and the oneness before God is more important than me getting my way, and it is more important to another getting their way.

That's just the way God designed it to work. So, if there's a problem in the marriage, the first thing you need to understand is to get closer to God because there's a basic submission aspect. The roles of husbands loving wives and wives submitting to husbands will undo the natural animosity that is in that relationship. But the very first thing is to become one spiritually, to love one another as Christ loved us.

You see headship of Christ, you see Christ's submission to the

Father, and you see Christ's submission to mankind. What was the purpose of it? He makes it very clear in Ephesians 5.

> *For we are members of His body, of His flesh and of His bones. "For this reason, a man shall leave his father and mother and be joined to his wife, and the two shall become one flesh." This is a great mystery, but I speak concerning Christ and the Church. Nevertheless, let each one of you in particular so love his own wife as himself, and let the wife see that she respects her husband.*—Ephesians 5:30–33

What is Paul saying there? He is saying that the marriage relationship is a reflection of Christ's relationship to the Church. But in the marriage relationship between a man and a woman, they have natural animosity toward each other. The wife wants to control the man, the man wants to control the wife, and, in addition to that, they're both sinful people, so they have differences, and they seek self-will.

He says, "We are going to undo that, and they're going to become one unified entity that glorifies God." That's a picture of Christ and the Church. How is that a picture of Christ and the Church? I've got natural animosity towards God as a lost person. As a matter of fact, Scripture says that while you were yet enemies with God . . . what happened? Christ died for you.

Christ submits Himself to the Father, submits Himself to man to undo that, and to bring me to one with the Father yet again. Paul said, "This is a great mystery." What is the mystery? A mystery is something that is revealed in the New Testament that was not revealed in the Old Testament. In the Old Testament, the prophets could read those scriptures, and as they read those scriptures, they would read about a coming Messiah, and they would read about the whole world being one with God, the world of believers being one with God.

Gentile and Jew together—that was a mystery that was not revealed until you got into the New Testament. And so a mystery is not something mysterious; a mystery is something that is not previously revealed.

> *Of this salvation, the prophets have inquired and searched carefully, who prophesied of the grace that would come to you, searching what, or what manner of time, the Spirit of Christ, who was in them was indicating when He testified beforehand the sufferings of Christ and the glories that would follow.*—1 Peter 1:10–11

They would have read the scriptures, but they couldn't see how it was going to work together. They were searching carefully to understand when the events would happen. The Spirit of Christ within them was showing them, ahead of time, that Christ would suffer and that glorious things would come afterward.

When the angels rebelled against God, they were fixed in their state—the fallen angels will forever be fallen angels. The elect angels, or holy angels, will always be holy angels. God did not offer grace to them when they sinned. Some were fallen, some were holy, and it is going to stay like that. But what did He do with mankind?

Mankind rebelled against God, and what did God do? God sent a redeemer to bring those fallen people back into a right relationship with God. That's the mystery. How is God going to do that? Those Old Testament prophets would look at it and wonder how this could be? How could this take place?

When the Church comes, God takes Jew and Gentile and puts them together in one body. The marriage relationship is to reveal that. Jew and Gentile don't get along with God, because they're both fallen people, so God takes the Jew and brings him together with the Gentile and then brings them together one with the Father.

And He says marriage is a picture of that. Husband and wife don't get along, and there's also a natural animosity which parallels our animosity towards God in that relationship, so what is the Church, and what does the marriage show you? Man and wife can come together, and they can become one flesh, unified before God. The marriage is a reflection of the mystery of the Church.

A New Oneness

What did this bringing together do for us? Well, it radically changed man's relationship with God and man's ability to come before God.

> *You shall set bounds for the people all around, saying, 'Take heed to yourselves that you do not go up to the mountain or touch its base. Whoever touches the mountain shall surely be put to death. Not a hand shall touch him, but he shall surely be stoned or shot with an arrow; whether man or beast, he shall not live.' When the trumpet sounds long, they shall come near the mountain.*—Exodus 19:12–13

This passage is when the children of Israel get one of their first real introductions to God, when He gave them their Old Covenant. Moses gets instructions for the children of God to come out to the mountain because God is going to speak to him and give them their covenant, as well as look at the restrictions that are put on them. He sets bounds for the people all around.

Why must they take heed of the mountain? Because God is on the mountain. Man has to keep his distance from God. Not only can't you go up on the mountain, but you also can't even touch the mountain. You can't even get close to God.

This passage makes it clear that even if your dog walked up there and touched that mountain, you've got to kill the dog. You can't come near God. When the trumpet sounds long, they shall come near the mountain, but you're not going to touch it, and you're not going to come upon it. That was when the Old Covenant was given. That relationship has changed in the New Testament.

> *That which was from the beginning, which we have heard, which we have seen with our eyes, which we have looked upon, and our hands have handled, concerning the Word of life—the life was manifested, and we have seen, and bear witness, and declare to you that eternal life which was with the Father and was manifested to us—that which we have seen and heard we declare to you, that you also may have fellowship with us; and truly our fellowship is with the Father and with His Son Jesus Christ. And these things we write to you that your joy may be full.*—1 John 1:1–4

Those New Testament saints touched God. In the Old Testament, you couldn't even touch the mountain where God was, and in the New Testament, you can walk up and put your hands on God.

What a radical change! How did that change come about? That change came about because the Son submitted to the Father, the Son submitted Himself to man to bring about complete oneness and unity between man and God. We see how important submission was, that life was made manifest to us by Jesus Christ.

Because Christ submitted to the Father, and Christ submitted to man, He brought about the existence of a new oneness in relationship. What is the benefit of that?

> *Therefore, brethren, having boldness to enter the Holiest by the blood of Jesus, by a new and living way which He consecrated for us, through the veil, that is, His flesh, and having a High*

Priest over the house of God, let us draw near with a true heart in full assurance of faith, having our hearts sprinkled from an evil conscience and our bodies washed with pure water.—Hebrews 10:19–22

You see the difference in the relationship between the Old Testament and the New Testament.

Seeing then that we have a great High Priest who has passed through the heavens, Jesus the Son of God, let us hold fast our confession. For we do not have a High Priest who cannot sympathize with our weaknesses, but was in all points tempted as we are, yet without sin. Let us therefore come boldly to the throne of grace, that we may obtain mercy and find grace to help in time of need.—Hebrews 4:14–16

Once more, we see that He submitted to the Father, and He submitted to mankind. This entire passage is about man separated from God by sin and Jews separated from Gentile. But when Jesus Christ comes and submits to the Father and submits to man, He brings Jew and Gentile together and brings them into a loving relationship with the Father.

What do you have in marriage? It bears repeating. You have a man and a woman who are sinful and at odds with each other. Then, there's natural animosity put in there where the woman wants to control the man, and the man wants to control the woman, and God brings perfect unity back into that relationship. That relationship is to be a picture of Christ and the Church.

That's why marriage is so important. The angels look down at man and say, "How in the world is this happening, God? These people are rebelling against You. When we rebelled against you one time, we were forever evil or forever holy." God urges us to learn about His grace. We rebel against Him every day, and yet He still brings us back into oneness with Him.

And so, He says that is what the marriage is to be—that husband and wife have differences, and they have a natural resistance to each other, but because of grace, they can be one, and they can be unified together. God gives us the perfect plan to bring that about. That's what marriage represents.

How can you stay married for an entire lifetime? You work at it, right?

It's submitting to one another, and it is understanding your roles in that relationship, because we're working together to bring glory to God. We are illustrating to the world what the grace of God is in a relationship, and we're going to show the world what the grace of God is. Just like we see that through the work of Christ, as the angels look at it, your marriage is an illustration to the world around you.

Two sinful people can get along—people who would have major differences in this life, and because of their relationship with Christ, they can get along and become one. We can become the unified force that God intended marriage to be. That's why submission is so important. Christ submitted to the Father, Christ submitted to man, and during that whole time, He was never anything less than He was before.

He is equal to God. There's no difference between a man and a woman in the eyes of God. Women are on just as solid a spiritual ground with God as men are, and a woman is no less than a man is in their relationship with God. There are places in the Bible where the Scripture says we're no longer man and no longer woman. But this is talking about believers, in that relationship that God establishes.

Christ could be in perfect oneness with the Church, and a husband

and wife can be in perfect oneness with one another. That's a picture that God put together; that is the power that God gives us. And it is all done for what? For the glory of God and to illustrate to the world what God can do.

CHAPTER 4
Service
How We Are to Serve One Another

Wives, submit to your own husbands, as is fitting in the Lord. Husbands, love your wives and do not be bitter toward them. Children, obey your parents in all things, for this is well pleasing to the Lord. Fathers, do not provoke your children, lest they become discouraged.—Colossians 3:18–21

Understanding this passage means understanding that it is a part of a bigger context, which is this idea of putting on the new man. Back in verse 12, Paul tells us about the elect of God putting on tender mercies, kindness, humility, meekness, longsuffering, and how we are to bear with one another and forgive one another. We are urged that if we have a complaint against someone, we must forgive as Christ forgave us. Then He says to put on love and to let the peace of God rule in the reader's heart, to let the Word of Christ dwell in us richly. Whatever our words and deeds may be, they should be done in the name of the Lord Jesus Christ. In other words, our priority in life is to live for the Lord and to please the Lord.

From there, He talks about specific roles in a marriage relationship. But to fully understand the roles in a marriage relationship, there's something that predates this. In a Christian marriage, you have a Christian man and a Christian woman, joined in union. As we looked at before, first and foremost, we are brothers and sisters in Christ. In this chapter, we're going to look at the first of three priorities that need to be a part of our lives if we want to have a good marriage and to have a good relationship.

What are some of the priorities in the relationship of brothers and sisters in Christ? Namely, they are service, love, and humility.

Well, the first one we're going to look at is that of a servant. Why is service so important? Because it's one of the things Jesus models for us. We see an illustration of Jesus Christ washing the feet of His disciples. We know that Jesus is going to the cross to die, but before He goes to the cross to die, He takes His disciples into the upper room. They find a room, go up there, and have dinner together.

> *After that, He poured water into a basin and began to wash the disciples' feet, and to wipe them with the towel with which He was girded. Then He came to Simon Peter. And Peter said to Him, 'Lord, are You washing my feet?'*
>
> *Jesus answered and said to him, 'What I am doing you do not understand now, but you will know after this.'*
>
> *Peter said to Him, 'You shall never wash my feet!'*
>
> *Jesus answered him, 'If I do not wash you, you have no part with Me.'*
>
> *Simon Peter said to Him, 'Lord, not my feet only, but also my hands and my head!'* —John 13:5–8

The disciples are gathered together for this meal, and they sit down to eat. Contrary to the famous painting of the Lord's Supper, where everyone sits on the same side of the table in a chair, that is not how it happened. They were gathered in a circle around the table. A table in that day and time was about 12–18 inches off the ground, and they would sit on a pillow. They would lay their feet out to the side, and then the next person would lie in front of them on their pillow, and their feet would lie out as well. They'd be all the way around, reclining at the table.

Normal practice in that day and time and culture was that when they came into the house, there would be a basin by the door, and they would wash their feet. They came inside from walking in open street areas, which were dusty and dirty, covered with donkey and camel excrement on the ground. Walking in sandals, that stuff would get under their feet, and when they went to eat supper, no one wanted a pair of smelly feet right behind their head, so the normal practice was to wash the feet.

So in the upper room, we see Jesus and the 12 disciples, and the 12 disciples were already arguing about who was going to be the greatest in the kingdom. That was their goal. With that mindset, you could bet none of them were going to wash feet. That was out of the question. They might have even been saying to themselves, "It is better to have dirty feet than to sit down and wash someone's feet because I'm not a slave. Who do you think I am? I'm one of the 12. I walk with Jesus every day, so I'm not washing feet."

Then Jesus got up, took off His outer garment—he had an inner tunic on—and put a towel around Himself. Washing feet meant He would get dirty. After He got His inner garment dirty, He would have put His outer garment back on to look presentable.

So, wearing His inner garment, He got down next to the water and started washing their feet. He took the role of the lowest servant there; there was no lower service in that culture than to wash another person's feet. That was as low as you could get. That was the job of the house servant.

Then Jesus goes into this dialogue with Simon about this servanthood.

> *Jesus said to him, 'He who is bathed needs only to wash his feet, but is completely clean; and you are clean, but not all of you.' For He knew who would betray Him; therefore He said, 'You are not all clean.'*

> *So when He had washed their feet, taken His garments, and sat down again, He said to them, 'Do you know what I have done to you? You call Me Teacher and Lord, and you say well, for so I am. If I then, your Lord and Teacher, have washed your feet, you also ought to wash one another's feet. For I have given you an example, that you should do as I have done to you. Most assuredly, I say to you, a servant is not greater than his master; nor is He who is sent greater than He who sent Him. If you know these things, blessed are you if you do them.'*—John 13:10–17

Jesus is not saying, "From now on, anytime you get together, you need to wash each other's feet." No, He told them that what He did was an example to them. Despite being Lord and Teacher, He took the lowest role. In taking that lowest role, He demonstrated to them that one of the key critical functions in the Christian life is to serve other people. It's hard not to put yourself above others, but to put yourself below others... that flies straight in the face of what most people think of life in the world. It flies straight into the face of what most people think of marriage. Most people don't get into marriage to be lower than someone else. At the very least, they hope to be equal to their partner.

Finding Fulfillment

There was a couple I counseled before they got married. I've counseled with a lot of couples over the years about marriage, and responsibilities, and relationships. The key thing about marriage is that people will constantly come to me for marriage counseling and say, "I'm just not satisfied in this relationship. This relationship is not fulfilling; it is not meeting my desires. I'm unhappy." My basic, internal response is that it's a good thing. That is excellent. Because marriage was never designed to do any of that stuff. When people come into marriage, they have a misconceived idea of what marriage is.

Marriage is not going to fulfill your life, marriage is not going to make you content, marriage is not going to make you happy—it's just not going to do that. All those things are found in your relationship with Christ. If you come into a marriage relationship to get fulfilled, you're not going to be fulfilled. The two biggest needs that a person has in their life are to be loved and to know they matter. Those are the greatest needs that you have. But you don't come into a marriage relationship to be loved. And you don't come into a marriage relationship to know that your life matters or to have self-worth.

The only way you can find those is in your relationship with Jesus Christ. An imperfect person cannot meet those needs. So, when you come into a marriage, if your idea is that this relationship is going to make you content, this relationship is going to be fulfilling, this relationship is going to complete you, you are headed for a great disappointment. That's all there is to it.

Marriage is fulfilling. Marriage does bring happiness. Marriage does bring contentment, as long as marriage is approached the right way. And the right way is when a husband and wife come together. The goal in marriage is to remember that you are loved. You know that you matter because Jesus Christ died for you and to remember that greater love has no one than to lay down his life for his friends. Jesus gave up His life. For me, that is the greatest level and the highest caliber of love that you can have. I know that I matter because He died for me. I have worth and value because He delivered me from eternal separation from God. So, I have purpose.

The idea in a marriage relationship is that you come into that relationship to minister to the other person. The fundamental first step in a marriage relationship is the same thing in the Christian life. My function here is to serve them. That is my role. And you will find true fulfillment and happiness in marriage if you serve that other person, because when you fail to do that, you're not going to find contentment. You're not going to find happiness because you're looking in all the wrong places. You're not going to find it—true love is found in your relationship with Christ. True fulfillment is found in your relationship with Christ, not in other people.

When Jesus gives them this example and says that a servant is not greater than his master, He is making an argument from the greater to the lesser. Here He is, Lord and Master of the Universe, King of kings, Lord of lords. This is the night that He is going to be arrested, and He steps down and takes the role of the lowest servant that a person can be. In doing that, He gave us an example of what true Christian living is. If the master can step down to the lowest servant that there is, then what does that say about you and me? If the sinless Creator God over Heaven and Earth, who is about to go to the cross and die for the sin of the world, can take the role of a servant, why can't I?

Why can't you? That's the argument He's making here. Jesus slams the door on us and says our function and role is to serve. That is one of the key ingredients in the Christian life.

So, when we come into a marriage relationship, the idea behind a marriage relationship is that as a husband, you serve the wife, and the wife serves the husband. That's fundamental. It's easy to single out the parts of Scripture that mention women submitting. But, in a Christian relationship, you're serving each other, submitting to each other.

The Bible does not teach that you should lord over other people. God created man and woman in a perfect environment. He created Adam, and out of Adam, He wrought Eve using Adam's flesh and bone. It says He fashioned that woman, and He brought them together. And the two became one flesh. The two were set to be a unified force, to face the world, and to be an illustration of Christ in the Church. This is what unity can do. This is what togetherness can do. He said, *It's not good for the man to be alone. I'll make a helper comparable to him* (Genesis 2:18). He puts them in the garden, and they're unified, worshiping the Lord, until sin comes in and destroys that relationship.

When the Bible talks about the woman's desire for the husband, there is within the woman a natural desire to control that man, or to change him. I've often wondered why women marry the wrong man. I see it all the time. If we go back to the example of an eight-cylinder car, sometimes women choose a man who's not even a six-cylinder, with two cylinders jammed up. The turn indicators are missing. You might have bald tires on it, have a cracked windshield, a duct-taped dashboard, and she's thinking, "Well, I'm going to fix him. I'm going to change this dude into a prince."

You're not changing anything. You can't change a person. God can, but you can't. And people who get into those kinds of relationships come to me and say, "Preacher, this just isn't working." Well, no kidding. That's not how a marriage is supposed to be. A marriage is a man and a woman who love God and are focused on God in a relationship as a unified body, one flesh, conquering the kingdom for God. That's what God's design is. But because man sinned, there is a natural desire for the woman to control the man, and for the man to rule over her. That's not good either. That's why it's called a curse.

When you step into a marriage, there is that curse to constantly remind man that we rebelled against God. We want to see what it is like to have a rebellion, so He put it right in your relationship, and you have a constant reminder of sin every single day. Plus, you have just a natural fallen nature of man or the sin nature of man.

When you get into a marriage, you're putting two sinners together who have natural animosity toward each other. God says He is going to show us how to make this work. The first thing we deal with is the basic Christian relationship. Your husband is your brother in Christ; your wife is your sister in Christ. There are some basic things in that relationship that we do before we even talk about roles. And number one among those basics is to serve one another. Jesus Christ gives us the prime example of what service is—He stooped down to the lowest place that a person could stoop.

A Willingness to Serve

Then the mother of Zebedee's sons came to Him with her sons, kneeling down and asking something from Him.

And He said to her, 'What do you wish?'

She said to Him, 'Grant that these two sons of mine may sit, one on Your right hand and the other on the left, in Your kingdom.'

But Jesus answered and said, 'You do not know what you ask. Are you able to drink the cup that I am about to drink, and be baptized with the baptism that I am baptized with?'

They said to Him, 'We are able.'

So, He said to them, 'You will indeed drink My cup, and be baptized with the baptism that I am baptized with; but to sit on My right hand and on My left is not Mine to give, but it is for those for whom it is prepared by My Father.'—Matthew 20:20–23

Of course, we know the Sons of Zebedee abandon Jesus in the hour of His death, but they don't have a clue what their future actions will hold. After this exchange between Jesus and the mother, the other disciples were indignant toward the brothers. The other 10 disciples were listening to all of this, and they were mad because their moms weren't there to do the same for them. They were really bent out of shape, wishing someone would ask on their behalf.

And when the ten heard it, they were greatly displeased with the two brothers. But Jesus called them to Himself and said, 'You know that the rulers of the Gentiles lord it over them, and those who are great exercise authority over them. Yet it shall not be so among you; but whoever desires to become great among you, let him be your servant. And whoever desires to be first among you, let him be your slave— just as the Son of Man did not come to be served, but to serve, and to give His life a ransom for many.'—Matthew 20:24–28

There's our example. He did the ultimate service, giving His life up for people who want nothing to do with Him. But He said, if they—or we—want to be great in the kingdom of God, the way up is down. The way to greatness is to get low.

The hallmark of a Christian relationship is a willingness to serve others, not to gain from them. That is a fundamental, basic truth of the Christian life.

Therefore, whoever humbles himself as this little child is greatest in the kingdom of heaven.—Matthew 18:4

Whoever gets down low, that is the person who is really going to be up high. The goal in the marriage relationship is to try to out-serve the other person. It's the husband lifting the wife, and the wife lifting the husband. They don't speak badly about one another to others. But that's not the general view we have in marriages today. And why is that? Our basic tendency is self—What can I get? What is in it for me? What is my benefit? But in marriage, we are called to give.

Jesus, knowing that the Father had given all things into His hands, and that He had come from God and was going to God, rose from supper, and laid aside His garments, took a towel and girded Himself.—John 13:3–4

The three critical things at play here are that Jesus knew that God had given all things into His hands; He had come from God, and He was going to God.

So, before Jesus washes their feet, the Bible tells us He knew that He was Lord of all, Lord of lords, and King of kings. Jesus knew He had come from God. He came from the throne room of God down to earth. And lastly, He was going back to God.

If you had that on your plate, would it be hard to bow down to anyone? You better believe it would be, from a human perspective. We live in a world with people who say, "Do you know who I am?" when they're confronted. People want to lord their importance over other people.

"I'm the husband in this relationship. I'm busting my tail all day long to bring home a paycheck, and you don't appreciate that this is my house. This is my stuff."

Jesus owns the whole, created universe. He came from the throne room of God down here to Earth. And after He finished His work, He went right back up there. Jesus was seated at the right hand of the Father. When He came here to Earth, He said He didn't come to be served but to serve. He didn't come to lord over everyone; He came here to wash their feet. To give you an example of what true Christian living is, you see that Jesus came into the situation with full knowledge and understanding of who He was and is. And He still got down, yet again.

If Jesus Christ can do that, then a lowly sinner like me can surely do it. No one is above that because no one's ever going to rank that high. We must serve because that is the way of the kingdom. Remember, it is not for what you can get. It's because of what you've been given, and what has been commanded of you.

In a marriage relationship, a husband and wife must come into that relationship with the idea of serving each other. You and I must do what the Scripture says because it is not dependent on a reciprocal response. It's not dependent upon appreciation. It's not dependent upon recognition.

Whether your husband doesn't appreciate all you do, or your wife thinks you should be doing more, you're supposed to serve them regardless. We are to be a unified team for the Kingdom of God, which means becoming low.

When Jesus washed the feet of His disciples, what must have been going through their minds? "We should have done this. This man is about to lay down His life for the sin of the world. And He is down here washing our feet."

Jesus is the greatest servant who ever lived. There is no person who has walked the earth who has lived like Jesus Christ did. And there is no person who walked the earth who came from a more exalted position than Jesus Christ. He is the greatest of all who has ever lived. And if the greatest of the great can do that, then you and I can. Priority one in a marriage relationship is serving one another.

CHAPTER 5

Love

How Love, Humility, and Service Co-Exist in Marriage

A lot of times when we talk about marriage, we focus on the roles—wives submit to your husbands, husbands love your wives. I think a lot of times what we fail to do is address the front end of that. The front end of that in a Christian marriage is that your marriage partner, husband or wife, is a brother or sister in Christ first and foremost. The way you treat a brother and sister in Christ is the way you treat a husband or a wife, which comes before the roles. In marriage, there are two situations involved.

First, we're all sinful, and the Bible tells us that we've all sinned and come short of the glory of God. Even after we're saved, we still struggle with sin we still have moments where we get into the flesh. Christ solved that by going to the cross and dying for our sins, was buried, and raised again, and has given us the Spirit of God. There are basic relationship changes there, and when you're in the body of Christ, relationship with a brother and sister in Christ is a union; it is a family within a family. That deals with the sin aspect.

The other side of the coin is that when Adam and Eve fell in the garden, God put consequences on them that were ongoing to remind man of his sin. Those consequences being the desire to control one another.

What we are called to, however, is to serve one another. In the last chapter, we looked at this service. Now, we're going to talk about love.

How does love fit in the marriage relationship? We are not talking specifically about love for a husband and a wife, but about love in the Christian life and how that should be at the forefront of our relationships one with another.

> But concerning brotherly love, you have no need that I should write to you, for you yourselves are taught by God to love one another; and indeed you do so toward all the brethren who are in all Macedonia. But we urge you, brethren, that you increase more and more; that you also aspire to lead a quiet life, to mind your own business, and to work with your own hands, as we commanded you, that you may walk properly toward those who are outside, and that you may lack nothing.—1 Thessalonians 4:9–12

He talks about this love relationship between people in the body of Christ. It says here, "but concerning brotherly love." In the Greek text, that is one word, and the word is Philadelphia. It's a compound word coming from two Greek words—philos, which means beloved, dear, or friendly. The word philo is translated as love in Scripture. If you read your Bible, you see the word love is most likely going to be either philo, which means affectionate love, or it is going to be agape, which means an act of the will. Brotherly love is used five times in scripture, and this is one of them. The last half of that word, adelphas, is the Greek word for brother. Hence, we get the translation brotherly love. It means the type that is within a family or should be within a family. It's affection that you have for one another, a tighter bond.

You've probably heard it said before that blood is thicker than water. That's talking about brotherly love. You could fight with someone in another family, but chances are, their brothers will step up and help them, even if their brothers are at odds. They're going to come together against you. Why? Because of their strong sense of brotherly love. Families might argue and fight among themselves, but when you pick a fight with one member, you're picking a fight with the entire family. Take a look at America's history of feuds—probably the most famous being the Hatfields and the McCoys. That feud is a perfect example of the bond of brotherly love. The Hatfields and McCoys fought like cats and dogs within their own families, but if you were a McCoy going up against a Hatfield, or vice versa, you were in for a battle with the whole clan.

Brotherly love is that connection and the bond of a family. We see affection, care, concern, passion, a passionate type of love; it is a love that has feeling. Now you take agape love, which is an act of the will. Agape love is when I choose to love someone. There's no emotion involved in it. It's a choice that I make toward another person. For example, when the Bible says to love your enemy, the word used for love is not philo, it's agape. How do I love my enemy? We don't have feelings towards them. If we had feelings towards our enemy, chances are pretty good they wouldn't be our enemy. We don't have affectionate feelings for him, so what does it mean to have love for him? We are told in Scripture that if our brother is hungry, we should give him something to eat, if he's thirsty, give him something to drink. What is the principle behind that? Show common human decency towards that person. In other words, don't be vindictive, don't try to get revenge on him, just treat him with common decency.

We choose to agape someone, whereas a philo love means an affectionate, passionate, caring love. The Bible says we're to have that for one another. We see this throughout Scripture in five verses.

Be kindly affectionate to one another with brotherly love, in honor, giving preference to one another;—Romans 12:10

Let brotherly love continue.—Hebrews 13:1

Since you have purified your souls in obeying the truth through the Spirit in sincere love of the brethren, love one another fervently with a pure heart,—1 Peter 1:22

But also for this very reason, giving all diligence add to your faith virtue, to virtue knowledge, to knowledge self-control, to self-control perseverance, and to perseverance godliness, to godliness brotherly kindness, and to brotherly kindness love.—2 Peter 1:5–7

The way this word is used in these verses reflects a deep care and concern for the other person. It's about showing compassion and having a genuine, fervent desire for their well-being. In a marriage, a husband and wife should embody this kind of brotherly love toward each other. The affection we show our spouses should mirror the love we have for any other Christian believer.

However, in marriage, this love tends to be even more intense. In my premarital counseling, I often remind young couples that love and passion are essential in a marriage. It's crucial to understand that marriage is a significant commitment—it's a choice. You don't have to get married to live a fulfilling life, but if you do choose it, Scripture is clear: you must love one another.

A lot of times when I talk with young couples, I ask them why, if they can't even manage their own life, are they seeking to get into a relationship where they'll have to deal with another person? They would be better off getting their life together first before taking on more responsibility. Sometimes, it is better not to get into that relationship than to get into it and not really understanding the fullness of what is required. A marriage relationship requires us to minister to that other person. In order to do that, we have to get our own life together.

In 1 Thessalonians, Paul says, *but concerning brotherly love . . .* and then he says, *you have no need that I should write to you for you yourselves are taught by God to love one another.*

The word used for love at the end of that passage is agape. In one passage, we have both uses. We have brotherly love, and we have agape love. He says, "You don't have need for anyone to teach you this, but you need to love one another."

What does he mean when he says you don't have any need for someone to teach you this? When you come to faith in Christ, that establishes the relationship of brotherly love. That makes sense to you. In other words, the Holy Spirit of God brings that into the heart of a person. It is produced by God, and that is why it's so important to discuss Christian marriage, because in a Christian marriage, you're to first have brotherly love for one another. Paul says you don't have any need that I should teach you this—this is a common component in Christian relationship.

While speaking at other churches, I meet members of that Church and have conversations with them. The unique thing about meeting another believer in the Lord is that it is almost like you've known him for a while. There's already a relationship there. There's a brotherly love relationship.

The Spirit of God produces that in you. And that's what's so important about a Christian relationship. A lot of things in a Christian life, you don't need to be taught. They are provided to you by God, and this is one of those that is provided to you by God.

What does this mean and how does this function in our life to be taught this by God? How are we taught by God? First of all, when a person comes to faith in Christ, God brings your human spirit alive, and His Spirit comes inside of you. We call that a baptism of the Holy Spirit or receiving the Holy Spirit. It is the benchmark sign that a person is in a relationship with God.

In the Scriptures, particularly in Acts 2, Acts 8, Acts 10, and Acts 19, we see examples of people who, after coming to faith, received the Holy Spirit. These four instances represent distinct groups—Jews, Samaritans, Gentiles, and the disciples of John—who, after believing, were affirmed and validated by the apostles. These are unique experiences, and the reason I point this out is that many people today teach that when someone gets saved, they must then be baptized with the Holy Spirit.

In Acts 15, there's a meeting where Peter and the other apostles gather to address a debate in the early church. The issue at hand was whether someone had to first become a Jew—through circumcision—before they could trust in Christ and become a Christian. The apostles stepped in and essentially said, "Hold on—that's not true." If you look at the Scripture, that's not what they're teaching. We saw Gentiles come to faith in Christ, and they received the Holy Spirit just like we did, without ever becoming Jews. The clear sign, as shown in Acts 8, Acts 10, and Acts 19, was that they received the Spirit of God.

But you are not in the flesh but in the Spirit, if indeed the Spirit of God dwells in you. Now if anyone does not have the Spirit of Christ, He is not His. And if Christ is in you, the body is dead because of sin, but the Spirit is life because of righteousness. But if the Spirit of Him who raised Jesus from the dead dwells in you, He who raised Christ from the dead will also give life to your mortal bodies through His Spirit who dwells in you.—Romans 8:9–11

In this passage, he's referring to our position. When you place your trust in Jesus Christ, you move from being "in the flesh" to being "in Christ." Positionally, you are now in Christ, but your condition here on earth can change. You can either walk in the Spirit, living in close relationship with the Lord, or you can walk in the flesh. When you find yourself in the flesh, you can "rebound"—confess your sin—and return to walking in the Spirit. While your condition can shift between walking in the flesh or in the Spirit, your position remains secure. You are no longer in the flesh; you are in a completely new relationship—in Christ and in the Spirit. What this verse is telling us is that the presence of the Spirit in your life is the clear mark that you belong to God.

What does the Spirit of God do? What does Paul mean in 1 Thessalonians 4:9 when he says, *But concerning brotherly love you have no need that I should write to you, for you yourselves are taught by God to love one another.*

But the Helper, the Holy Spirit, whom the Father will send in My name, He will teach you all things and bring to your remembrance all things that I said to you.—John 14:26

This verse reminds us that one of the functions of the Holy Spirit is to teach us about God, and to bring to mind those things we should know. The primary context of that verse is to those disciples, but the application is also to you and me, because the Holy Spirit does teach us, and the Holy Spirit brings the remembrance of things we need to know. For example, it instructs us, "In that day and time, don't worry about what to say because my spirit will give you the Words to say."

If you've ever been talking to someone, and you might not have your Bible with you, it is amazing how you're able to draw scriptures out of memory. That's one of the ministries of the Holy Spirit.

God has always had a witness with His people. Old Testament used the Father, the Gospels used the Son, and after the death, burial, resurrection, and ascension of Christ on the day of Pentecost, the Spirit is with us. God is always with His people, and says the Spirit is our helper and will teach us all things and remind us of all the things the Father has taught.

> *However, when He, the Spirit of truth, has come, He will guide you into all truth; for He will not speak on His own authority, but whatever He hears He will speak; and He will tell you things to come.*—John 16:13

The Spirit of God instructs us—that's why Paul said in 1 Thessalonians 4:9, *But concerning brotherly love you have no need that I should write to you, for you yourselves are taught by God to love one another.* Brotherly love comes with the Spirit of God in our life. There's a natural affection for other believers now.

> *But you have an anointing from the Holy One, and you know all things. I have not written to you because you do not know the truth, but because you know it, and that no lie is of the truth. Whoever denies the Son does not have the Father either; he who acknowledges the Son has the Father also.*

> *Therefore let that abide in you which you heard from the beginning. If what you heard from the beginning abides in you, you also will abide in the Son and in the Father. And this is the promise that He has promised us—eternal life.*

These things I have written to you concerning those who try to deceive you. But the anointing which you have received from Him abides in you, and you do not need that anyone teach you; but as the same anointing teaches you concerning all things, and is true, and is not a lie, and just as it has taught you, you will abide in Him.—1 John 2:20–27

There are some basic fundamental things that the Spirit of God teaches us, but for other things, God uses teachers to do that. We are taught both ways, by the Spirit of God and by teachers. He says here that we have an anointing.

For years, people taught that you had to receive an anointing by God to be able to do something well. The Scripture says that you already have an anointing from God. You have the Spirit of God in your life, you have this anointing from Him, so you need to get it out of your mind that there are some Christians that are superior to other Christians because of some special anointing in their life. Some Christians are very gifted, some Christians are very talented, some Christians yield in a greater capacity to the Holy Spirit, but all Christians have the same equipment.

We have all the tools necessary for the Christian life. It's just that we have to learn how to utilize them. Just like in baseball, those guys all have the same equipment. Some of them are a lot better with that equipment than other ones. That guy on the bench is playing back up, but he's got the same equipment. That guy starting, he just utilizes the equipment better. Christian life is like that, but all Christians have the same equipment. There's no category of super Christian—there's no such thing.

We have a lot of false teaching in our churches today and Christian ministries that teach that you lack what you need for Christian life.

God says in 2 Peter, "I've given you all things that pertain to life in godliness." God has equipped us to live the Christian life. And this "anointing" people teach about is the same thing.

The phrase "abiding" in this passage refers to something that is ongoing. When it speaks about the anointing you receive that "abides in you" and "teaches you," it's in the present tense, indicating a continuous action. This anointing doesn't stop; it remains with you. When you come to faith in Christ and the Holy Spirit enters your life, you are given an anointing from God to be taught and to learn His ways. So, what is the role of a teacher then?

> *And He Himself gave some to be apostles, some prophets, some evangelists, and some pastors and teachers, for the equipping of the saints for the work of ministry, for the edifying of the body of Christ, . . . —Ephesians 4:11–12*

There are two basic things that the Spirit of God teaches you. One of those things is brotherly love, there are basic fundamental things in the Christian life that you learn from God. Second, you have pastors and teachers that exegete the Scripture and teach you about the things of God. But the real teaching takes place when the Spirit of God takes that teaching and applies it. In both cases, you're still being taught by God.

The Bible says the natural man cannot receive the things of the Spirit of God, so to receive anything from God, you have to have the Spirit of God in your life. To understand it, you have to have the Holy Spirit teaching you. The reality is that the Holy Spirit is only going to teach you what is accurate and true to what the teacher tells you.

You can believe anything you want, but that doesn't mean it is coming from God. God has given us the Word of God. We have to take everything that we are taught and run it through the Word of God. We have to find out if it's of God or not. I don't care how influential, or handsome, or powerful or "anointed" the teacher is, if it doesn't square with the Word of God, we don't need it. We have to bounce things off of God's Word, because only God honors His Word. If you believe a falsehood in your life and you live out that falsehood, you will suffer consequences from it. So how does the Holy Spirit teach us?

When I teach the Word of God, the Holy Spirit illuminates it, and by illuminating the Word of God, He makes it understandable to us. In that process, the Holy Spirit is teaching us the truth about God, so God teaches us how we should maintain a relationship one with another. In a relationship, between a husband and wife, they're both Christians, so there's brotherly love in that relationship—that's first and foremost.

There's a misconception in marriage that the way you behave toward your spouse is somehow different from how you treat others in Christian relationships. Some people think it's acceptable to speak harshly to their spouse, criticize them, or condemn them. But there's no allowance for that. How you treat your spouse reflects how you treat God. How can you say you love God, whom you can't see, and yet harbor hatred for your spouse, your brother or sister in Christ? This is crucial to understand. Often, the intensity of conflicts in a marriage can become more passionate than in other relationships, but that doesn't give us a pass to mistreat one another. In a marriage, it's vital to remember: "I need to treat my wife as I would treat my sister in Christ—with kindness, respect, and affection."

That predates the rules we tend to want to go to, the rules where a wife's role is to submit to the husband and the husband's role is to love the wife. Before that, they were brother and sister in Christ, and they need to be serving each other. They need to be loving each other in that relationship.

This love at the end of the passage in 2 Peter is agape love. He is using both in the same passage, so how does that work in a relationship? Our love, affection, care, and concern towards someone many times is based on performance. When they're doing what I like, we get along great, but when they don't do what I like, or they mess up or they fail, we don't get along. What the Bible says is to love your wife as Christ loved the Church. And the Church didn't love Him back. The Church didn't perform well, but He said I love you, and I love you so much I'm going to lay down My life for you. I'm going to die for you. Therefore, in a marriage, a husband's love for his wife should be based on her position in the relationship, and the wife's love for her husband should be based on his position. Not their performance.

A lot of conflict in marriage comes about because love is given based on performance, and that kind of love is selfish. It's selfish because we always say we're not getting what we want out of this relationship. If we're feeling unfulfilled or unhappy in a relationship, what we're really saying is that we're not loving the other person with agape love. Instead, we're expecting something in return from the relationship. But we can't expect perfection from imperfect people. When we do, we're setting ourselves up for disappointment.

We get preconceived ideas in our minds, and then when reality doesn't live up to it, and we're disappointed. If you come into a marriage and your preconceived idea is that the husband is going to make you happy, complete, that life will be great and fulfilling—quit watching soap operas and fairy tales. We're talking about a real live man. That person is going to disappoint you, let you down, and be imperfect, but when that happens, and we don't have that burning desire, that's when we exercise agape love. We love our spouse based upon their position, and when you love like that, the affection will come back because your role in a marriage relationship is not what you can get out of it, it's how much can you put in there.

Agape love is, I love you based on your position, brotherly love is that strong affection, care, and concern for that other person that predates anything related to roles in a marriage relationship.

My number one rule in a marriage relationship is to come in and serve that person you're married to, and their responsibility is to serve you. But even if they don't serve you, remember those disciples didn't serve Jesus in that upper room, but He kept washing their feet, didn't He? He kept cleaning them, just like in brotherly love. Serve that person and care for that person, without the thought of anything in return.

The world has so infused the teaching on marriage that it becomes very confusing. I don't know where this idea came from about how we're supposed to be satisfied and fulfilled in a marriage relationship. You can only be satisfied and fulfilled one way, and that's your relationship with Jesus Christ. He loves you with a perfect love, and you matter because He laid down His life for you. When those two basic needs are met, you don't need to get that from another person, and you can't get it from another person. If you go into a marriage and understand your responsibility is serving that person well, that is what marriage is. Marriage is giving 100% to each other. The man gives it to a woman, and the woman gives it to the man. The advantage you have is that you're a Christian, in a Christian marriage and you have God living in you both, therefore you have all the tools necessary to make it work.

CHAPTER 6
Humility
How to be Humble in Marriage

Not that I have already attained, or am already perfected; but I press on, that I may lay hold of that for which Christ Jesus has also laid hold of me. Brethren, I do not count myself to have apprehended; but one thing I do, forgetting those things which are behind and reaching forward to those things which are ahead, I press toward the goal for the prize of the upward call of God in Christ Jesus.

Therefore let us, as many as are mature, have this mind; and if in anything you think otherwise, God will reveal even this to you. Nevertheless, to the degree that we have already attained, let us walk by the same rule, let us be of the same mind.—Philippians 3:12-17

These are basic Christian characteristics that we should be putting on in our lives to live for the Lord. I've summarized these in three areas—service, love, and humility. In this chapter, we're going to look at humility as a foundation in marriage.

Let nothing be done through selfish ambition or conceit, but in lowliness of mind let each esteem others better than himself. Let each of you look out not only for his own interests, but also for the interests of others.—Philippians 2:3-4

As we look at this passage, we keep marriage in mind. We're to serve one another in marriage, despite the inherent sin nature that arose in the garden and the friction it caused between man and woman.

We looked at the passage of Scripture where Jesus Christ served the disciples by washing their feet on the night before His execution on the cross. He humbled Himself in their sin, but first He served them. He essentially said, "I'll leave you an example so that you serve one another."

The first rule in a marriage is that a husband and wife should serve each other.

The second rule is to love one another—both with agape love (selfless, unconditional) and philos love (affectionate, brotherly).

The third rule is humility.

These principles address the core issues of sin in our lives. The roles within the marriage are influenced by the fall: when Adam and Eve sinned in the garden, God came to them and established certain consequences that now affect our relationships.

God is now bringing man and woman back into a unified team. That's how He wants it to be. There's a lot of false teachings on marriage and relationships today. One of the big issues that is spoken of a lot is that women are to submit to their husbands. That's exactly what Scripture says. But what does that mean? What does that look like? Well, it's recognition of position in a relationship. Jesus Christ submitted to the Father, and the Holy Spirit submits to Jesus Christ. There's no diminishing of Deity there. There's no diminishing of personal worth. The same thing is true in a marriage relationship.

To submit means to rank in line; it means for each person to fulfill their role or their responsibility. When God created the woman, she came alongside man as a helpmeet, and they work together as a team. They move forward against the forces of evil in the world, seeking to glorify God. The Scripture is undoing all the things that sin did.

In Philippians 2:3, Paul says, *Let nothing be done through selfish ambition or conceit.* The phrase "let nothing" means there is no area of our life that should remain outside of God's control. Many people believe that there are parts of our lives we live for God and other things we do for ourselves. However, this is not true. Every aspect of our lives should be lived for God. So much so that the Scripture even says in I Corinthians 10:31, *So whether you eat or drink or whatever you do, do it all for the glory of God.* Eating and drinking are essential for life. You have to eat, and you have to drink. They are the most basic means of survival, but God saying that even in the most trivial, unrecognized areas of life, we must do it for the glory of God.

How do I eat, and how do I drink for the glory of God? That's a question that you have to ask yourself. You eat and you drink to glorify God when the number one priority in your life is God. When you prioritize your relationship with God, everything you do in life is done to fulfill that relationship with God. You're not doing it for yourself. You're doing it for God. I eat so I can have energy to serve God. I drink so I can be hydrated in my service to God. Whatever I do, in every area of my life, I do for the glory of God. Let nothing, not one thing in your life, be controlled by selfish ambition or conceit.

What is Selfish Ambition?

In the New Testament, the Greek word often translated "selfish ambi-tion" means "work for hire," describing someone motivated only by personal gain. Another way to phrase it is, the person is a hireling. What is hireling? A hireling is a person who's in the job just for the paycheck. He is just in it for money. He doesn't care one way or the other. It's all for him. Another word that has a similar meaning is the word mercenary. What does a mercenary do? A mercenary hires out to a foreign power to conduct war for them for the sole purpose of money and personal gain.

Selfish ambition is one that seeks its own way. It's an inordinate self-love, self-gratification. Selfish ambition lives with complete disre-gard for the rights and feelings of others. It means to be a self-wheeled person. What is the downside of selfish ambition? The downside to selfish ambition is that it is a source of strife and contention in a per-son's life. If you were to go back and read the book of First Corin-thians, you would see it clearly. What was the basic problem in the Church at the core? Selfish ambition and conceit were the basic prob-lems. Whenever you have selfish ambition, you're going to have strife and conflict.

If we have selfish ambition in our lives, we're not going to get along with other people, because we're going to be constantly putting ourselves first over that other person. We're never going to take second place. We're always going to be pushing ourselves out in front. That is a basic desire in all human beings. It's not unique to the person you're married to. It's a condition that is in every human being on the face of the earth. The very essence of sin is self.

The very essence of sin is to put self before God and to put self before others. That's what tends to drive our life from our flesh. The other word he uses here is conceit. The word *conceit* is a compound word as well. The word *canas* means empty, and the word *doxy* means glory. Whenever you see the word glory in the Bible, it's the word *doxy*. *Doxy* and *glory* here would be self-praise.

Philippians 2:3 says, *Let nothing be done through selfish ambition or conceit.* Some translations say *empty conceit.* That is a better translation of the word because the actual word that is used there is the word *empty glory.* Another way to phrase it would be vain glory or empty praise. It is the exalting of natural man who is devoid of good over anything that is good. It is seeking self-praise, a person who has a highly exaggerated self-view. The person who has vain conceit never struggles with self-esteem.

> *I wrote to the church, but Diotrephes, who loves to have the preeminence among them, does not receive us. Therefore, if I come, I will call to mind his deeds which he does, prating against us with malicious words. And not content with that, he himself does not receive the brethren, and forbids those who wish to, putting them out of the church.*—3 John 9-10

This person that he's talking about here, Diotrephes, was a person who was driven by vain conceit, or self-conceit. The Bible warns about this in numerous places.

> *Do not be wise in your own eyes; Fear the Lord and depart from evil.*—Proverbs 3:7

> *Do you see a man wise in his own eyes? There is more hope for a fool than for him.*—Proverbs 26:12

> *Woe to those who are wise in their own eyes, And prudent in their own sight!*—Isaiah 5:21

Be of the same mind toward one another. Do not set your mind on high things, but associate with the humble. Do not be wise in your own opinion.—Romans 12:16

Lowliness of Mind

What's the difference between selfish ambition and empty conceit? Selfish ambition seeks personal goals. It is the desire to have your own way. If you can seek, seek personal glory. One is, is your willpower, and the other one is seeking self-glory. In verse 3, he says, *"Let nothing be done through selfish ambition or conceit . . ."* but that's a contrast. Instead of seeking my own goals, instead of seeking my own glory, what should I do? *". . . in lowliness of mind, let each esteem others better than himself."* Paul is saying that instead of seeking my own way, instead of seeking my own glory, I should seek that for other people. Put other people above yourself, humble yourself, and put them in that position. Build other people up and help them get to the top.

This concept of lowliness of mind was never used in secular Greek writing. The Greeks and the Romans had nothing to do with lowliness of mind. The culture of the Greeks and Romans was that self is first. When Paul writes this, he's writing counter-culturally.

American culture demonstrates the same thing. What do TV commercials promote? *You deserve the best. You deserve a break today. Come to our store, and you can have it your own way.* Everything is geared to feed into that. People who are good at marketing or advertising, they feed the selfish ambition of others because they know it's what sells.

Look at most of the magazines that are out there. They exalt the self, and they exalt the lives of Hollywood celebrities, which are the gutter filth of the earth for the most part. These people live in debauchery and evil, and yet they are exalted. They're looked upon in our culture as being models for everyone else to look at. Most of them can't maintain a relationship. Most of them are constantly at odds with other people. They're consumed with greed and all kinds of stuff, yet what does our culture do? Our culture will write magazines about them because people want to read about their lives. After people read about them, they emulate them. That's the general mindset of culture.

And so, it's only natural that it feeds over into our personal life, because that's what everyone around us is doing. It's very easy to fall into that trap. Many times in a marriage relationship, you'll hear people say, *I'm not happy. I'm not fulfilled. I'm not being treated right. I'm not being recognized. I'm not being appreciated.* Why? Because the basic mindset is, *I should be in this relationship, and I should be getting all that stuff.*

That's never a promise we are given in Scripture about a relationship. Anytime you put two sinful people together, there will be conflicts. You compound that with a curse that is on the marriage relationship because of the man's sin, and there will be outright combat behavior going on. How do we step in as believers and fix that? God has given us the guidelines to do so. But the first area He addresses is our personal sin. He says lowliness of mind will lead each of us to esteem others better than ourselves.

Andrew Murray said, "Lowliness of mind means you don't even have a thought about yourself. You just put that out. You forget about having your way."[1]

---

[1] Murray, Andrew. Humility (Updated Edition). Cet.2. New Kensington, USA: Whitaker House, 1982. Text.

Also, He spoke this parable to some who trusted in themselves that they were righteous, and despised others: 'Two men went up to the temple to pray, one a Pharisee and the other a tax collector. The Pharisee stood and prayed thus with himself, "God, I thank You that I am not like other men—extortioners, unjust, adulterers, or even as this tax collector. I fast twice a week; I give tithes of all that I possess." And the tax collector, standing afar off, would not so much as raise his eyes to heaven, but beat his breast, saying, "God, be merciful to me a sinner!" I tell you, this man went down to his house justified rather than the other; for everyone who exalts himself will be humbled, and he who humbles himself will be exalted.'—Luke 18:9-14

Pharisees were the top religious leaders of that day. Pharisees sought to protect the Word of God. They sought to protect the Church. They were very legalistic in their approach to life. They made very sure that when they were out in public, everything they did was to project an image of righteousness—that they were better than everyone else. If you saw a Pharisee, you would know he was a religious man. You would think they did everything God said to do. You would view them in a favorable light. You would look at them as being very religious people. But Jesus said, *they're full of dead men's bones.*

What about the tax collector? A tax collector was one of the lowest people in society. A tax collector collected money from the people for the Roman government. The Jews viewed the Roman government as being evil. So, a tax collector would be viewed in much the same light as a low-life type of person. If you were standing there, and Jesus started with this first sentence, "*Two men went up to the temple to pray, one a Pharisee and the other a tax collector,*" you would say, "Oh, a Pharisee. I'm on his side because he's a good guy." In that culture, he was viewed as the good guy. The tax collector was viewed as a scumbag, and no one liked him. But rather than saying a good prayer, the Scripture says the Pharisee was speaking to himself. What is the very essence of prayer? Talking to God? God didn't receive that prayer. This parable infers that he's just bragging on himself. What would that be called? Selfish ambition and conceit.

The tax collector, however, is standing far off. He would not so much as raise his eyes to heaven, but he beat his breast, saying, *"God be merciful to me, a sinner."* The conclusion is clear. The tax collector is justified, rather than the other. Why? *Everyone who exalts themselves will be humbled, and he who humbles himself will be exalted (Luke 18:14).*

God honors those who humble themselves, but God does not honor those who exalt themselves. If you exalt yourself, God's going to bring you down. But if you humble yourself, God will lift you up.

Selfish ambition can come in several ways. Some people use it in a very dominating way. They want to be first, to be recognized. Some people use it another way, and they use it to say they're not being treated right, with proper respect. That is selfish ambition in the reverse order. But in both cases, it's a person seeking themselves, which is in opposition to what God says.

Humbling Ourselves

One of the first concerns that pops into my mind is that if I humble myself, people are going to take advantage of me. If I put myself low, somebody is going to step on me and squash me. You hear that a lot of times in a relationship.

What does God say? You humble yourself, and God will exalt you. God will take care of it. It is a matter of faith. It's a matter of trusting God to deal with that other person in your relationship. God deals with all sin. He doesn't tolerate any sin. We have to be concerned with obedience rather than results.

> *But Jesus called them to Himself and said, 'You know that the rulers of the Gentiles lord it over them, and those who are great exercise authority over them. Yet it shall not be so among you; but whoever desires to become great among you, let him be your servant. And whoever desires to be first among you, let him be your slave—just as the Son of Man did not come to be served, but to serve, and to give His life a ransom for many.'*—Matthew 20:25-28

Here's Jesus Christ, creator of heaven and earth, sovereign over-all, the most powerful being that exists. When he comes to earth, he doesn't come to be served. What does he do? He comes to serve others.

From the greater to the lesser, Jesus Christ, who is Lord of heaven and earth, took on a human body, then humbled Himself to the point of death, and went to the cross. If he can do that, surely, we could do that towards other people. Selfish ambition and conceit are common in all of us. If we get into a marriage relationship and we're driven by selfish ambition and conceit, we will not have a unified marriage. The husband and the wife will each be seeking their own way, and that pre-dates the roles in a relationship. We're to serve one another, love one another, have humility towards one another, and not seek to be first.

I see it illustrated on a daily basis with my two dogs. One dog is older than the other dog, but they're both small Border Terriers—excellent riders and excellent hunters. But when I go to let the older dog out the door, he always wants to be first. We previously had another dog that we lost. When we had our other dog and this older dog, the older one would jump over the other one to get out the door first. He wanted to be first in everything. But we lost the other, and I got a puppy. That little puppy is driven by selfish ambition to the 10th degree over the older dog. His entire life revolves around selfish ambition.

So, when I go to let them out the door, it's kind of funny because sometimes they both will jump at the same time and bump each other in the air when they try to go out the door. They're battling to be first. I know they're both going to get out the door. It doesn't matter if one is in front of the other, but I can't get that Christian discipline into their life because they constantly battle for the door. They'll even start biting each other because they want to get out the door first. That's exactly what we do in life. We want to get our way, so we'll fight and battle over insignificant, trivial things in life. And what does it do? It creates strife and conflict. But God always sides with the lowly. God always sides with the poor. God always sides with the disadvantaged. That's how God is. God is a champion of the person on the bottom.

I will praise You with my whole heart;
Before the gods, I will sing praises to You.
I will worship toward Your holy temple,
And praise Your name
For Your lovingkindness and Your truth;
For You have magnified Your word above all Your name.
In the day when I cried out, You answered me,
And made me bold with strength in my soul.
All the kings of the earth shall praise You, O Lord,
When they hear the words of Your mouth.
Yes, they shall sing of the ways of the Lord,
For great is the glory of the Lord.
Though the Lord is on high,
Yet He regards the lowly;

But the proud He knows from afar.
Though I walk in the midst of trouble, You will revive me;
You will stretch out Your hand
Against the wrath of my enemies,
And Your right hand will save me.
The Lord will perfect that which concerns me;
Your mercy, O Lord, endures forever;
Do not forsake the works of Your hands.—Psalm 138

He comes alongside the lowly. He backs away from the prideful. Wherever we come up short, God will fill it in. God will lift us up. If we humble ourselves, God will lift us.

Likewise, you younger people, submit yourselves to your elders. Yes, all of you be submissive to one another, and be clothed with humility, for

'God resists the proud,
But gives grace to the humble.'

Therefore, humble yourselves under the mighty hand of God, that He may exalt you in due time, casting all your care upon Him, for He cares for you.—1 Peter 5:5-7

This Scripture teaches us that when we humble ourselves, God will lift us up. All we have to be concerned with is being obedient to what the Scripture says. God will fulfill the rest. We're concerned that others will take advantage of us, but God says to just get low, and He'll lift us high.

In our marriage relationships, if we would commit to serve one another, and to love one another, and if we would be humble as we approach one another, we could resolve 99% of the problems that surface in a relationship. Treat each other with humility, love, and service, and put ourselves on the bottom. That's what marriage is really about.

The marriage relationship is the husband ministering to the wife, and the wife ministering to the husband. That's the biblical model. It's easy to preach and teach, but hard to apply. We have to look at it every day, and we have to commit anew to it and remind ourselves because that's what God wants us to do. Jesus humbled Himself to the point of death, and God has exalted Him above every name, that in the name of Jesus, every knee will bow, and every tongue will confess He is Lord. God calls it obedience in humility.

CHAPTER 7
Rules and Roles
The Role of Submission

After looking at service, love, and humility, it's time to consider how we display them in the marriage union. We see the act of fulfilling our roles as a way to bring the team back together and have a unified front. One of those roles is the role of submission.

Wives, likewise, be submissive to your own husbands, that even if some do not obey the Word, they, without a word, may be won by the conduct of their wives, when they observe your chaste conduct accompanied by fear. Do not let your adornment be merely outward—arranging the hair, wearing gold, or putting on fine apparel—rather let it be the hidden person of the heart, with the incorruptible beauty of a gentle and quiet spirit, which is very precious in the sight of God. For in this manner, in former times, the holy women who trusted in God also adorned themselves, being submissive to their own husbands, as Sarah obeyed Abraham, calling him lord, whose daughters you are if you do good and are not afraid with any terror.

Husbands, likewise, dwell with them with understanding, giving honor to the wife, as to the weaker vessel, and as being heirs together of the grace of life, that your prayers may not be hindered.—1 Peter 3:1-7

They're a team—a husband and a wife are heirs together. They are partners in this relationship. It's not that one's in charge and the other one's a servant; they both work together as a team. For that team to work right, God gives us specific guidelines. He says wives are to submit to their own husband. In the passage, the word for submit is *hupotasso*. It's a compound word—*hupo* meaning under, and *tasso* meaning to arrange in order.

Hupotasso is primarily a military term. When used as a military term, it means for everyone to fall into their rank position. I was in a leadership position in the Marine Corps as an officer and had several platoons. But in that platoon, I had a staff sergeant. That was my platoon sergeant. Then I had squad leaders who were sergeants. Everyone had a position to fulfill in that arrangement.

Somebody had to make the final call. Someone had to make the final decision that was going to take place. And in the case of a platoon, it was me. But see, even me, in my position, I was under authority. I had a captain who was the platoon commander I had to answer to. But that captain wasn't free to make any decision he wanted. That captain had a battalion commander he answered to. And even that battalion commander wasn't free—he had a regimental commander he answered to. The regimental commander answered to the division commander. The division commander answered to the assistant commandant, the assistant commandant to the commandant, commandant to the president. You see, nobody is really free. And the president? He answers to the people in our form of government.

Everyone's under authority. Everyone has an authority in their life. But the idea behind the military was to channel everything to where you had functional units. In its non-military use, the word *Hupotasso* means to give in and cooperate.

Hupotasso is seen as respect and willingness to serve another. That's the idea behind the word. In a lot of modern churches, there is somewhat of an understanding that a woman is under the man, that he's in charge, and she had better submit.

This brings us back to Genesis 3, where it is stated that man desires to rule over the woman. It emphasizes that within their relationship, there is a divinely appointed order, with God choosing the man to lead because Adam was created first. This reflects the created order: Adam was formed first, and the woman was made from Adam.

One person will have to answer (Hupotasso), but they work together as a team. There are other usages of this term in the Bible to help us understand it.

For to be carnally minded is death, but to be spiritually minded is life and peace. Because the carnal mind is enmity against God; for it is not subject to the law of God, nor indeed can be. So then, those who are in the flesh cannot please God.—Romans 8:6-8

The carnal mind is in opposition to God; it is inherently against His will. The word "subject" in these verses is *hupotasso*, which means to submit or align under authority. The carnal mind does not obey God's law or cooperate with it; instead, it operates independently of it. However, when the carnal mind submits to the law, it is no longer operating in its natural, sinful state but is instead functioning in a way that reflects the mindset of the Spirit, since the carnal mind cannot submit to God's law on its own.

Brethren, my heart's desire and prayer to God for Israel is that they may be saved. For I bear them witness that they have a zeal for God, but not according to knowledge. For they, being ignorant of God's righteousness, and seeking to establish their own righteousness, have not submitted to the righteousness of God.—Romans 10:1-3

In these verses, we see that Israel does not submit to God's righteousness. They were trying to use their own righteousness. They said they had their own rights, and they were self-righteous with their own rules. But Paul tells them they need to submit to the righteousness of God. In other words, put yourself under and in agreement with the righteousness of God.

I urge you, brethren—you know the household of Stephanas, that it is the first fruits of Achaia, and that they have devoted themselves to the ministry of the saints—that you also submit to such, and to everyone who works and labors with us.—1 Corinthians 16:15-16

He is saying that, within the body, both those who serve and those who lead must submit to one another, be in agreement, cooperate, and work together harmoniously.

Jesus Models Submission

"Then He went down with them [His parents] and came to Nazareth, and was subject to them, but His mother kept all these things in her heart."—Luke 2:51, author's emphasis

Again, the word *subject* here is *Hupotasso*.

Did Jesus's parents rule over Him? No. Not at all. This passage is saying Jesus was subject to them. But understand—at no point was Jesus less than fully God. Instead, in this passage, the creator of the universe is submitting to sinful human parents because that's the right thing to do.

If Jesus can do that with His parents, can't a wife do that with her husband? What does that mean? *He submitted to them*? Jesus came to earth and took on a human body. And He functioned on earth as a Jewish male. Number one, He fulfilled the law and, in fulfilling the law, there was not one jot or tittle of the law that was left undone. He submitted Himself to the law of God. Even though He wrote it, He put Himself under it.

At the same time, He submitted to His parents and put Himself under them. He was in agreement with them. I don't know what it would be like to be the earthly father of Jesus. I wouldn't want that position. But because Jesus fully submitted, He could point out how spiritually ignorant various decisions were. As His earthly father, you couldn't win the argument. But what did He do instead? He put Himself under the authority of His parents, because that is what He was supposed to do as a young male. That's the idea. That's the same word that is used in Colossians for *wives submit to your own husbands*.

The idea of the wife submitting to the husband is the same thing as Jesus submitting to His parents.

All that the Father gives Me will come to Me, and the one who comes to Me I will by no means cast out. All that the Father gives Me will come to Me, and the one who comes to Me I will by no means cast out. For I have come down from heaven, not to do My own will, but the will of Him who sent Me.—John 6:37-39

Jesus was subject to His parents, to the law, and to the will of His Father. When He came to earth, He operated in that capacity. He said, *I didn't come to do my own thing. I came to fulfill the will of the Father.* In the Godhead, Jesus is equal with the Father, and the Holy Spirit is equal with the Father and Jesus in the Triune God. There's no difference in those three. They're fully God. Yet to fulfill the specific plans of God, the Son says, *I will put myself under the authority of the Father,* and the Spirit will put Himself under the authority of Christ. That's what submission is. Submission is to work in respect and willingness to serve another.

Submit is a present-tense word. In Colossians, where it says wives submit to your husband, the present tense means it's a continual action. It means it is something you do continually. It's in the imperative mood—meaning it's a command. It's also in a middle voice. That means that you do it yourself. It's not the husband's job to make the wife submit. It's the wife doing it continually because it's commanded. It's not commanded by the husband; it's commanded by God. The wife works in agreement with the husband because that's what God has commanded her to do. They work as a unified team in that relationship to fulfill the law of God.

An important note about this passage is that it's only applicable to her relationship with her husband. The wife, the woman, does not submit to another man. It's only in the marriage relationship that the woman submits. Why? Because God says you do it with your own husband. That's the command. You stay in agreement with your husband. You show respect to your husband because that is the relationship you're in, and that's the plan God has established. He wants man and woman in this relationship working as a team.

It's like a football team. You get all the players on the football team, and you've got this one guy they call the captain of the team.

What does the captain do? He does the coin toss; if they are on the field during a penalty, they are typically the one who communicates with the referee about accepting or declining the penalty. But when it comes to running the team, what does he do? He works in conjunction with the rest of his teammates.

The same thing is true in a marriage relationship. A husband and wife work together as a cohesive unit for the glory of God. But when it comes down to it, the man is responsible for what goes on there because that's the way God has established it. That's the way God has set it up.

It says *wives submit to your own husbands as is fitting to the Lord.* What in the world does that mean? The word *fitting* is the word *necho*, which means proper or correct. A *necho* is an obligation. When the passage says, *wives submit to your own husbands as is fitting*, it is followed by *in the Lord*. This is a prepositional phrase to tell you where. He's telling you to submit your own husbands as is proper and correct, and your obligation because of your positioning under Christ Jesus. It is a basic responsibility to honor God by doing this. It's not because the man deserves it, it is not because the man requires it, because he doesn't. It's because the Lord requires it. It's because the Lord says so that it's proper and correct in your relationship with God to do this, to submit to the husband. To submit means to be respectful and willing to serve.

Don't ever forget that the primary responsibility in a marriage relationship is two people together who have to counteract sinfulness. I'm not in this marriage for myself. This relationship may not bring me happiness. It may not bring me joy. But show me one place in Scripture where sinful things are going to bring you joy, contentment, and happiness. No husband on this earth can do that. There's not a woman on earth who can do that. So don't think that when you get married, all those needs are going to be met. Those things are only met by the Lord.

In a marriage relationship, the husband works to minister to the wife, and the wife works to minister to the husband. That's the opposite of sin. It's not your wife's job to please you. Pleasure is a decision you make in life, whether you're pleased or not. And if your pleasure is built upon the performance of somebody else, what you need is a trained monkey. You don't need a wife; you need a poodle to perform for you. That's never God's plan in a marriage relationship. All that thinking does is create and demonstrate to us our own selfishness.

Every time we get displeased or we get unhappy, it should be a reminder. What do you put your hope in? Your hope is never to be put into man. Your hope is to be put into God. Your fulfillment is to be found in God. Your completeness in life is to be found with God. Why would you substitute it with something simple?

Getting our Priorities Straight

Everything I have in life is2 found in the person of Christ. Seek first the Kingdom of God and His righteousness, and all these things will be added unto you. Pursue God with all your heart, with all your mind, and with all your soul, and your life will be complete. So you've got to get your priorities right. But instead, we get our priorities wrong, and then we say, "I'm not happy in life because of them."

When God walked in the garden, He said, "Adam, what did you do?" He said, "That woman that you gave me made me eat the fruit of the tree." And so God said, "Woman, what did you do?" She said, "Well, that serpent made me do it." See the natural tendency of man, the reflection of sin and man is to blame other people for our problems. When we get into a marriage relationship, we start blaming everything on our spouse when the problem is us. We're the one who's the problem, because we're putting our hope into the wrong thing. So when you talk about a marriage relationship, a husband and wife together, the idea that the husband is ministering to the wife, the wife is ministering to the husband, and they both have responsibilities fulfilling that relationship.

Ephesians 4:1-3 urges us to live a life that is worthy of our calling, meaning we are to live up to the standard set for us. When we are born again, we are in Christ Jesus, and we are called to walk in a way that reflects this truth. What is our calling? We are saints of God, born of Him, and seated with Him in the heavenly realms. Therefore, our lives should align with the position we hold in Him.

The verses show us how to live in humility. That means not demanding our own way. It's putting myself below that other person and saying, "What do you want in life, and how can I support that?" The idea is to come back into oneness, as husband and wife in that relationship.

The passage in Colossians discusses how the wife should submit to her own husband and how that is fitting in the Lord. You do it because it's a command from God. A wife submitting to her husband is obedience to God. It defines the reason for it. Why should you do it? It's not because your husband is a good guy. It's not because your husband is a good leader. It's not because your husband is smart or good-looking. You submit to your husband because that is your obedience to God.

Submission is not slave subordination, but rather that you recognize and support him. You come alongside him. The husband's responsibility, which we will discuss in the next chapter, is to demonstrate love back to that wife instead of ruling over her.

The biggest problem we have in society today is a direct reflection of the family. Politicians will blame society's failures on everything in the world, and everyone thinks the way to fix it is more money. But the only way we're going to fix society is when families get it right, because families set the tone for the whole culture.

We have a representative republic as our form of government, meaning people have freedom. Our founding fathers said that without a moral conscience, free men cannot exist together. Where are morals and righteousness taught? They're learned in the family. You get some in church, but the basic idea is a husband and wife tending the garden for God, nurturing and bringing their children up in the Lord. As you model unity before the children, and you guide the children, it's the family unit where children learn respect, honor, decency, and all these basic moral fundamentals in life. But if you look at the world around us, most families allow a culture to run their home. They allow the media to run their home. They allow Hollywood to run their home. They get their guidance for life from soap operas and movies.

Go back fifty years, and you get shows like Dick Van Dyke. They had the husband and wife sleeping in separate beds because they didn't think it was appropriate for them to share. I agree that's prudish because my wife isn't sleeping in another bed. I want her with me. But that's not the issue at hand. Back then, they weren't willing to put anything with an immoral appearance on television.

Today, we've allowed shocking behavior from shocking people to dictate our culture to us. Yet many Christians embrace culture more quickly than they embrace the Word of God. They let culture define how a marriage should be. They let culture define how a man should be. They let culture define how a woman should be. They let culture define how children should be. And look at the chaos we're dealing with today. When people in our society enjoy freedoms without a moral compass to guide them, they lack the proper foundation to make wise decisions. They're not being led by the power and Spirit of God, nor is their conscience shaped by Him. The only way to transform our society is by first transforming our families.

Consider the profile of the average inmate in the prison system. Close to 80% of them have an unknown father or no contact with the father. I've read probably 300,000 inmate profile cards in my time, and I can tell you that it's common. You could take the profile of the average inmate, replicate it, and apply it to any of them with just a few minor adjustments, because the pattern is the same. The default is often no father, limited or absent fatherly involvement, and a troubled home life. And that's just the beginning.

Many are exposed to drugs and alcohol at a young age, and this contributes to a troubling pattern that paints a very clear picture. When young children don't receive proper guidance at home, they often learn from their parents and from the surrounding culture. And as this cycle continues, the culture itself begins to spiral. So, how do we fix this? The solution starts with re-establishing the home. It begins in your own household—through your relationship with your children, your family, your grandchildren, and your nieces and nephews. You must model what it looks like for a husband and wife to live together in harmony, working as a team and reflecting the glory of God to those around them. This is what marriage is meant to be: a reflection of Christ's relationship with the Church. And how does Christ love the Church? With a sacrificial, unending love.

How obedient is the Church? Not every. Every day we have to confess sin. Yet God's love never changes. God's love is always there. That's how marriage is to be. That husband isn't always going to please you; that wife isn't always going to please you, but you've got to forgive one another even as Christ forgave you. You've got to live in that unified relationship because the next generation is dependent on it.

More important than anything, honoring God must be done every day. And that's why the family is so important. That's why it's so criti-cal for a husband and wife to understand and define their role. What's my responsibility as a husband? My responsibility is to lead my family to know God and deliver God to them, and my wife is right alongside me, helping me to do that. There's no diffusion of the message. It's a unified team pushing in that direction, fighting against culture and the rotten, corrupt mindset that envelops us in life.

We are rising above that and pushing through to produce champi-ons who will raise up a family and do the same thing. It's passing that heritage down the line. That's God's plan for the family. The family is the spearhead of humanity. It sets the tone for everything around us. You lose the family, you lose the culture, you lose the fear of God. You have to reach the family and put them where God says they should be. Deal with your sinfulness and understand what your responsibility is in this relationship. My responsibility as a man is to love my wife as Christ loved the Church. My wife's responsibility is to respect and to work with me to force and purge and push forward for the glory of God, to tend our part of the garden, to take care of our life, and she's there to help me do that.

And when we do that, we live in victory. It doesn't matter what's going on around you; you'll have peace and joy and all the fruit of the Spirit in your life. Why? Because you're living the way God designed for you to live. You don't need the external trapping. What you need is an internal heart, focused in the right direction.

CHAPTER 8
A Hard Husband
How Submission Works through Difficult Times

What should a woman do when dealing with a difficult man? We want to exercise marriage the way God designed it, where a husband and wife become one flesh, live together, and are a united team working for the glory of God. A woman works to respect the man; the man loves the woman. There's a harmonious relationship, and the whole purpose behind that is to reverse the curse that is currently on the marriage relationship.

We see a problem in the case of Abigail in I Samuel 25, who has a very hard-headed man whom she tries to deal with. How does she make an appeal? How does she resolve conflict? The principles are applicable to us in how we can resolve conflict in a relationship.

Now there was a man in Maon whose business was in Carmel, and the man was very rich. He had three thousand sheep and a thousand goats. And He was shearing his sheep in Carmel. The name of the man was Nabal, and the name of his wife was Abigail. And

she was a woman of good understanding and beautiful appear-
ance, but the man was harsh and evil in his doings. He was of the
house of Caleb.

"When David heard in the wilderness that Nabal was shearing
his sheep, David sent ten young men; and David said to the young
men, "Go up to Carmel, go to Nabal, and greet him in my name.
And thus you shall say to him who lives in prosperity: 'Peace be
to you, peace to your house, and peace to all that you have! Now
I have heard that you have shearers. Your shepherds were with us,
and we did not hurt them, nor was there anything missing from
them all the while they were in Carmel. Ask your young men, and
they will tell you. Therefore, let my young men find favor in your
eyes, for we come on a feast day. Please give whatever comes to your
hand to your servants and to your son David.'

"So when David's young men came, they spoke to Nabal according
to all these words in the name of David and waited.

"Then Nabal answered David's servants, and said, "Who is David,
and who is the son of Jesse? There are many servants nowadays who
break away each one from his master. 11 Shall I then take my
bread and my water and my [c]meat that I have killed for my
shearers, and give it to men when I do not know where they are
*from?—*1 Samuel 25:2-10

Abigail was a wise woman, knowledgeable, and beautiful. But the
man, in contrast, was harsh and evil. So you've got a woman of understanding, a woman who, according to Scripture, has a godly character.
She's also beautiful, and she's married to a man from the house of
Caleb who is very harsh.

David is traveling with about 600 of his men, fleeing from Saul, who is trying to kill him. Nabal is shearing what is likely thousands of sheep. David is on the brink of becoming king of Israel, but he has no intention of claiming Saul's authority.

David had interacted with Nabal's shepherds as the shepherds traveled across the plains, showing them kindness. David's men didn't steal sheep to feed themselves, and they treated the shepherds well. In fact, one of the shepherds even mentioned that David's men had defended them at times, acting as a protective wall against those who would cause trouble.

Now, David is asking for Nabal's help to feed his 600-man army, requesting that they share some of the food that is plentiful during this feast time. His request is entirely reasonable. His men approach Nabal and present their appeal.

However, they were rejected and disrespected. They made their appeal, but Nabal spoke to them in a harsh, rough manner. He was very rude in the way he spoke to them, and Scripture says that David's men turned on their heels.

So David's young men turned on their heels and went back; and they came and told him all these words. Then David said to his men, "Every man gird on his sword." So every man girded on his sword, and David also girded on his sword. And about four hundred men went with David, and two hundred stayed with the supplies.

"Now one of the young men told Abigail, Nabal's wife, saying, "Look, David sent messengers from the wilderness to greet our master; and he reviled them. But the men were very good to us, and we were not hurt, nor did we miss anything as long as we accompanied them, when we were in the fields. They were a wall to us both by night and day, all the time we were with them, keeping

the sheep. Now therefore, know and consider what you will do, for
harm is determined against our master and against all his house-
hold. For he is such a scoundrel that one cannot speak to him.
—1 Samuel 25:11-17

It's well known that Nabal is a very harsh individual. He is a man
who stirs up strife, like we read in Proverbs 15:1. David's coming after
him with 400 men, and David's going to chop him into pieces. And so
this shepherd goes in and tells Abigail what went on.

Then Abigail made haste and took two hundred loaves of bread,
two skins of wine, five sheep already dressed, five seahs of roasted
grain, one hundred clusters of raisins, and two hundred cakes of
figs, and loaded them on donkeys. And she said to her servants, "Go
on before me; see, I am coming after you. But she did not tell her
husband Nabal.

So it was, as she rode on the donkey, that she went down under
cover of the hill; and there were David and his men, coming down
toward her, and she met them. Now David had said, "Surely in
vain I have protected all that this fellow has in the wilderness, so
that nothing was missed of all that belongs to him. And he has
repaid me evil for good. May God do so, and more also, to the
enemies of David, if I leave one male of all who belong to him by
morning light.

Now, when Abigail saw David, she dismounted quickly from the
donkey, fell on her face before David, and bowed down to the
ground. So she fell at his feet and said: 'On me, my lord, on
me let this iniquity be! And please let your maidservant speak
in your ears, and hear the words of your maidservant. Please,
let not my lord regard this scoundrel Nabal. For as his name is,

so is he: Nabal is his name, and folly is with him! But I, your maidservant, did not see the young men of my lord whom you sent. Now therefore, my lord, as the Lord lives and as your soul lives, since the Lord has held you back from coming to bloodshed and from avenging yourself with your own hand, now then, let your enemies and those who seek harm for my lord be as Nabal. And now this present which your maidservant has brought to my lord, let it be given to the young men who follow my lord. Please forgive the trespass of your maidservant. For the Lord will certainly make for my lord an enduring house because my lord fights the battles of the Lord, and evil is not found in you throughout your days. Yet a man has risen to pursue you and seek your life, but the life of my lord shall be bound in the bundle of the living with the Lord your God; and the lives of your enemies He shall sling out, as from the pocket of a sling. And it shall come to pass, when the Lord has done for my lord according to all the good that He has spoken concerning you, and has appointed you ruler over Israel, that this will be no grief to you, nor offense of heart to my lord, either that you have shed blood without cause, or that my lord has avenged Himself. But when the Lord has dealt well with my lord, then remember your maidservant.'
—1 Samuel 25:18-31

I don't think for a minute that Abigail ran into the kitchen and whipped this dinner up really quick. She had a wide variety of servants there, and they were loading down a caravan. She made a plan.

What's Abigail doing here? She's interceding for Nabal. David and his men are angry and hungry. Plus, his pride is hurt. David is acting in vengeance. David's a man of war. He's fought all his life. When he was a young man, he protected his father's sheep, he defended the flock against lions, and he defended his flock against bears. A short time after that, he beat Goliath, and now he's leading the armies of God to take out people when God directs him to do so. When he hears that Nabal has rejected him for food, he wants to make him pay. And so David has armed his men, they've put on their swords, and they're headed towards Nabal.

Abigail is also reminding David not to worry, that he will be king one day anyway. So why the need for vengeance over this?

Then David said to Abigail: 'Blessed is the Lord God of Israel, who sent you this day to meet me! And blessed is your advice and blessed are you, because you have kept me this day from coming to blood-shed and from avenging myself with my own hand. For indeed, as the Lord God of Israel lives, who has kept me back from hurting you, unless you had hurried and come to meet me, surely by morning light no males would have been left to Nabal!' So David received from her hand what she had brought him, and said to her, 'Go up in peace to your house. See, I have heeded your voice and respected your person.'

Now Abigail went to Nabal, and there he was, holding a feast in his house, like the feast of a king. And Nabal's heart was merry within him, for he was very drunk; therefore she told him nothing, little or much, until morning light. So it was, in the morning, when the wine had gone from Nabal, and his wife had told him these things, that his heart died within him, and he became like a stone. Then it happened, after about ten days, that the Lord struck Nabal, and he died.

So when David heard that Nabal was dead, he said, 'Blessed be the Lord, who has pleaded the cause of my reproach from the hand of Nabal, and has kept His servant from evil! For the Lord has returned the wickedness of Nabal on his own head.'

And David sent and proposed to Abigail to take her as his wife. When the servants of David had come to Abigail at Carmel, they spoke to her, saying, 'David sent us to you, to ask you to become his wife.'—1 Samuel 25:32-40

Many people think that Nabal was paralyzed. He possibly had some kind of a stroke because the word scared him so badly.

Principles from Abigail and Nabal

This is a story of a godly woman who is married to a scoundrel, according to Scripture. He creates a very difficult situation, and yet she shows respect for her husband in spite of the fact that he's not very deserving of it. There are some principles we can draw from here because you may be a woman who is married to a very harsh man, or maybe be married to a man who is a scoundrel. It happens. So how do you deal with it? Well, let's look at some principles from this text.

Principle number one is this. Conflicts in a marriage relationship are inevitable. They're going to happen. Anytime you put two people together, there's going to be conflict; there's going to be discord. Whether it's related to our own singleness or in the case of marriage, it's related to the fact that in marriage, the woman wants to control the man, and the man wants to control the woman. When conflicts exist, and even when the situation is bad, understand that God is still there. Just because the situation is bad, doesn't mean you run away from what God says because it's a bad situation. This situation is bad, but the Word of God says He will never leave us nor forsake us.

We have to operate according to biblical principles to deal with this situation. If I operate out of my flesh, that's what David did. He was going to avenge this whole thing Himself because he was angry. Many times when we get into a situation and a conflict arises, we go outside the parameters of God and know what we're going to do, and when we do that, we're going to create a bigger problem. We'll reap as a result of it in the end.

Abigail is a woman who operates with the understanding that God is with her. And so she puts together a plan of what she needs to deal with.

The second principle is that when confronted with the problem, Abigail dealt with it. That's a principle right there. Abigail dealt with it. Abigail had several options here. Option one: she could let Nabal be. She could just let it be and let David have his vengeance. Option two, she could have been controlled by fear. David's angry, her husband's angry, and she's afraid of what's going to happen, and she does nothing. And then option three is, she could just play it off. You know how Nabal is. He's just like that, and there's nothing to be done.

But she doesn't do any of those things. What does she do? She understands what the need is, and she provides for the need—the food. She goes and makes an intercession to David on behalf of her husband. She deals with the problem.

When a problem comes up in a relationship, ignoring it or playing it off, or letting it play out many times, is not the way to go. The best way to deal with the problem is in a biblical manner. I can assure you, because Abigail was a woman of understanding, she was praying. She was praying a lot about what was going on the journey because she had no idea what was going to take place.

One of the first steps you take, once you decide to do something, is to cover it with prayer. You pray and ask for God's intercession and for God to help. You operate in accordance with God's Word.

Lastly, Abigail goes, and she speaks. But note, when she speaks, she speaks from the position of humility. A woman who honors her husband seeks to calm the situation, not create a bigger situation.

A calm answer, a soft answer, turns away wrath. She interceded, and she dealt with it in a calm and stable way. If we let our emotions take over, or let our anger take over, a harsh answer stirs up strife. We end up creating a bigger problem. But another principle we see here is that Abigail is submissive in a relationship with a difficult man. She didn't make excuses for Nabal. When she went to David, what did she say? She said, *"David, my husband is a scoundrel."* She's not running him down. She's just stating what the case is; she's just stating the truth. Abigail isn't trying to minimize what Nabal is. She's just stating the truth while trying to correct the wrong. She's respecting him, but she's interceding for him at the same time.

After she resolved that problem by talking to David, she went back to Nabal. And what did she see? When she got home after going through all this trouble, there's Nabal drunk. It says that she withholds her comments until the wine has left him. See, a wise woman not only will deal with a situation in humility, but she'll choose the proper time to deal with it, and she doesn't react in anger.

What would have happened had Abigail just said, *"Nabal, you're drunk. That's all you ever do. You're a hard-headed old man, you're a drunk, and look at all the problems you've created."* What result would that have had? It would create a bigger issue. It would create a bigger problem. But what does she do? She backs away from the situation, waits for the appropriate time, and makes an appeal with humility.

Abigail's purpose in confronting both Nabal and David was not to escalate the situation, but to prevent a bigger conflict. She wasn't seeking revenge, but aiming to resolve the issue. In difficult relationships, we should strive to be peacemakers, working to resolve the problem rather than using the situation to tear the other person down, which is exactly what Abigail does not do. Instead, she steps in for her husband, even though he is undeserving of it, to address the issue. Often, people may not deserve something, but we show them respect by helping to ease the burdens they face. However, it's important to approach such situations with the right timing, the right language, and the right preparation.

Abigail was a godly woman who was more concerned about others than she was about herself. She was concerned about Nabal because he was hard-headed, made stupid decisions, made careless comments, and put himself in a position where a whole group of people were about to be crushed because of him. David was coming for Nabal and all of his men. But Abigail saw through all of Nabal's foolishness, and she took action.

The final principle is that God honors humility. The Scripture tells us that God resists the proud, but He gives grace to the humble. A way to resolve a difficult situation is to exercise humility and operate in accordance with the Word of God.

In the end, Abigail was blessed. Nabal was off the table, and David married her, and they lived together, and she had children from David. We know of at least one that she had with him. But we see how to deal with a difficult situation. The key principle is that a soft answer turns away wrath. It's all about the approach and the way you deal with something. She doesn't rehash the whole story; she just lays out the facts, and she deals with it in a manner that expresses humility. We can learn from that.

So, if you're dealing with a difficult person, prepare, take it before God, and pray. Wait for the appropriate time to respond, and when you respond, respond with humility, and have the motivation of heart to resolve the issue, not to create a bigger issue. That's how you resolve conflict. So, if you're dealing with a difficult person, exercise those principles to approach it, and let God work through the midst of it.

Remember, no matter how challenging the situation may be, God is still present, and you can always turn to Him. God does not tolerate ignorance or the behavior of scoundrels like Nabal, nor does He put up with stubborn, rebellious people. If you seek God, allow Him to work, and approach the situation with humility, patience, and a willingness to wait for the right timing, you will often see God move in the midst of it, bringing resolution.

CHAPTER 9
The Role of the Husband
How a Man is to Behave in Marriage

Husbands, love your wives and do not be bitter toward them.
—Colossians 3:19

As we continue this study through Colossians 3, we move from the role of the wife to the role of the husband. The word here for love is the Greek word *agape*, which we already said means unconditional love or a sacrificial love that results from an act of the will. When he makes this statement, he uses the present tense, active voice, imperative mood. That means it's to be a continual action. There is never a time when the husband is allowed not to love his wife. It's a perpetual thing. It is a continual love that is demonstrated to the wife by sacrificial service that comes about through an act of the will. Active voice simply means it is a choice that we make. We choose to love.

As an imperative, it means it is commanded of us. When a husband loves his wife as Christ loved the Church, he is being obedient to God. A man who is married to a woman cannot be obedient to God if he doesn't actively love his wife. Out of obedience to God, he must continually love her, sacrificially.

If my natural tendency is to rule over my wife, how can I do something like that? We looked at putting off the old man and putting on the new man.

If you go back and look at verse 14 of the same chapter, it says, *"And let the peace of God rule your hearts to which you are called in one body and be thankful."* Remember, the word *rule* means *empire*. The peace of God in our hearts is an empire that lets us know when we're out of bounds. If we don't have the peace of God, if we have anxiety or guilt in our life, then the peace of God is not ruling in our life. It tells us we got something wrong, and we need to go back and check it.

Then it says, *Let the Word of Christ dwell in you richly in all wisdom. Teaching and admonishing one another in Psalms and hymns and spiritual songs. Singing with grace in your heart to the Lord.* This is one of the prison epistles of Paul. He wrote Galatians, Ephesians, Philippians, and Colossians while in prison. There's a parallel passage of this in the book of Ephesians.

> *And do not be drunk with wine, in which is dissipation; but be filled with the Spirit, speaking to one another in psalms and hymns and spiritual songs, singing and making melody in your heart to the Lord, giving thanks always for all things to God the Father in the name of our Lord Jesus Christ, submitting to one another in the fear of God.*
>
> *Wives, submit to your own husbands, as to the Lord. For the husband is head of the wife, as also Christ is head of the Church; and He is the Savior of the body. Therefore, just as the Church is subject to Christ, so let the wives be to their own husbands in everything.*
>
> *Husbands, love your wives, just as Christ also loved the Church and gave Himself for her, that He might sanctify and cleanse her*

with the washing of water by the Word, that He might present her to Himself a glorious Church, not having spot or wrinkle or any such thing, but that she should be holy and without blemish.— Ephesians 5:18-27

Instead of letting wine control you, let the Spirit control you. The word *filled* means to be controlled by. Let the Spirit of God control you, and look at the output of that. The phrases, *filling with the Spirit* and *the Word of God dwelling in you richly,* are synonymous. When He says for husbands to love their wives, He's saying you must do this through the control of the Spirit of God. The spirit of God is what sets the table for you. That's why the title of this section is called Christian marriage.

Christians have the Spirit of God and, therefore, they have enablement to do this. We, as men, have the ability to continuously, actively love our wives in obedience to God. We don't love based on emotions, feelings, or desires of the heart. We don't love based on performance. We don't base our love upon outcomes. The love that we have is an act of the will to the choice that we make. We do it as we are controlled by the Spirit of God. Loving your wife is also parallel with another passage of Scripture.

But when the Pharisees heard that He had silenced the Sadducees, they gathered together. Then one of them, a lawyer, asked Him a question, testing Him, and saying, 'Teacher, which is the great commandment in the law?'

Jesus said to him, 'You shall love the Lord your God with all your heart, with all your soul, and with all your mind.' This is the first and great commandment. And the second is like it: 'You shall love your neighbor as yourself.' On these two commandments hang all the Law and the Prophets.'—Matthew 22:34-40

The second half of that commandment, *love your neighbor as yourself,* is a normal Christian responsibility. We have a basic relationship with our spouse in a Christian marriage where our spouse isn't just a spouse. My wife is also my sister in Christ. So, I'm going to love her as I would love myself. We have a double love that is in there. We love her in just the relationship of being a Christian, but we also love her based on her position in the relationship as a wife. It's clear as you look at Scripture that these commandments can only be carried out through the power of the Spirit. My natural inclination, along with every man, is self-first and to control the wife. Get your wife under control. That's the culture. That's what we hear. And if we're not careful, as men, will let culture drive our relationship versus letting Christ drive it. We are to be Christ-driven as believers.

Loving your wife is an act of your will. I had a friend when I was in seminary, and we went to eat lunch one day. While we were eating lunch, he asked me if I'd ever fallen out of love with my wife. I said, "No, I haven't. Why?" He asked again, and I replied the same. I told him I didn't ever fall in love with my wife. That's a cultural use of the word love. It's like a hole in the ground or a trap—you just walk along and all of a sudden you fall, and you're in it. But that's not real love. Love is an act of the will.

I didn't know that when I met my wife. I was 16. She was 15. I made up my mind. "That's the one I want right there." It took a while, and it took some patience and persistence, too, but I got her in the end.

It was seven years later before I came to faith in Christ. She was saved six months after me, and it was a whole different ballgame. It's a ballgame that I'm still active in, that I'm still learning. I still fail all the time at that, but it doesn't change the truth. The truth is, love your wife sacrificially and continually as an act of your will. When you love your wife, it is a choice that you make and continue; it never ends. That means making adjustments in our lives. It means doing things that we might not want to do, going against our natural, sinful nature. Acting in obedience to the Word of God means submitting to the Spirit of God.

But the critical thing about the home is that it's incumbent upon us as husbands and wives to bring up the next generation, that they will love their wives and that their wives will respect their husbands. That's how it's pushed forward. It's a continual thing. We're one generation away from losing any sense of order and discipline in our society. And so, we have a responsibility as men to lead in that relationship to demonstrate what true Christian marriage looks like.

The Five Functions of the Husband

Marriage has become attacked in our culture—it's in a state of disarray. It's treated as something that's disposable, that's second-hand, that's not important, and yet God spends time in His Word explaining to us how that relationship is to work. Therefore, it's extremely important. And we need to value it in the same way if we want to bring up another generation of godly people. We have to pass that torch on to the next generation. And one of the ways we do that is for husbands to love their wives sacrificially, as Christ loved the Church.

Sacrificial love, in these verses, is laying down personal desires for the betterment of another. And that's exactly what the Lord did. But the other side of the coin is this: men by nature are leaders, just by nature. That's what men are, that's how men were created from the moment God placed him in the garden and said, "*. . . Let us make man in our*

image, after our likeness: and let them have dominion (Genesis 1:26).
Men are basically hunters and protectors. That's been a responsibility.
Whether you look at tribes in Africa, whether you look at native Amer-
ican culture, whether you go back and look at European culture, that's
the way men are wired, men are to be leaders. They are to take the lead.
God has put them in a position of leadership.

But leadership can come in a variety of forms, too. I read a book
about leadership, and then in that book, he gives about 12 different
models for leadership. He says, there's an ego leader, there's the selfish leader, there's a narcissistic leader, to name a few. So just because
you're leading in a home doesn't mean you're leading in the right way.
What is the correct model of leadership? If I'm going to be a leader
in my home, what model of leadership should I have? Well, I take it
that the highest form of leadership out there, the most effective form
of leadership, is what we call servant leadership. That is the leadership
that Jesus Christ has for His Church. And we're told to love our wives
as Christ loved the Church. So as Christ loves the Church, Christ also
leads the Church.

And how does Christ function in the Church?

- Well, number one, He leads the Church.
- Number two, He has a presence in the Church.
- Number three, He has provision for the Church.
- Number four, He has protection for the Church.
- And number five, He promises good for the Church.

So, we're going to look at all five of these over the next few chapters, and we're going to begin with how a man should lead, how he
should lead in his marriage, and how he should represent Christ.
How do we do that? We should follow the same pattern and the same

model as Christ, and Christ's style of leadership is referred to as servant leadership.

We already looked at Matthew 20, when the mother of James and John asks Jesus if her boys can sit at his right and left side in Heaven. The other disciples were not pleased. Imagine when she made that request, those heads were whipping back and forth. But Jesus brings them all around Him and tells them that whoever wants to be first will be a servant. Jesus's style of leadership is servant leadership. He leads the Church, but He does it with the heart of a servant. He led those disciples with the heart of a servant.

Likewise, the style of leadership for a husband is to be a servant leader. A servant leader serves the people whom they lead, and the people willingly follow because they will identify with that. Servant leadership is what I was taught in the Marine Corps, and servant leadership is the biblical model that has been put forth. If a husband is to love his wife like Christ loved the Church, they are to leave the days of men sitting back and being idle and passive. It's going to have to come to an end. Men are going to have to take leadership, but they don't lead as tyrants. They don't lead as a control freak—that kind of leadership is going to be rejected.

The style of leadership that men must have is servant leadership. Servant leadership means laying down my life for the betterment of others. So, if someone's coming after your family, it's where you put yourself down in front of them. And I'm not only talking about a physical attack or someone shooting your family. I'm talking about when they try to warp the minds of your children or warp the mind of your wife. The culture we live in seeks to destroy what is good and proper and what is right and forthright—a man must lead through servant leadership.

Some things are inherent within servant leadership. First, servant leadership must understand the needs of those they lead. To be an effective leader in a servant model, you've got to understand the needs. In the military, those basic needs were to make sure the men are fed, make sure the men have water, make sure the men have the equipment they need, and so on. You inform them. You meet every need that they have. That is your responsibility. You take care of your people.

In a marriage relationship, a man must understand the needs of his wife.

> *Husbands, likewise, dwell with them with understanding, giving honor to the wife, as to the weaker vessel, and as being heirs together of the grace of life, that your prayers may not be hindered.*—1 Peter 3:7

When you fail to understand your wife, and when you fail to deal with your wife in a proper manner, your prayers are going to be hindered. In other words, it has a direct conflict with your spiritual life. So, dwell with understanding. That's the model that Christ gives us.

> *Therefore, do not be like them. For your Father knows the things you have need of before you ask Him.*—Matthew 6:8

When Christ leads us, He knows what needs we have. It's inherent upon us, as men, to find out what the needs of our wives are. And the way to do that is to ask what she needs.

The second point on servant leadership is you don't request the wife to do anything that you would not do. That's basic in servant leadership. In the military, they taught us, you don't make your man do anything that you wouldn't do. That was pounded in our heads.

Every time you go out on patrol, you have to have what is called a point man. The point man's responsibility is to be the first guy in the line on the patrol. So, if he's walking, he's the first guy who's going to hit booby traps. He's the first guy who's going to see the enemy; he's usually the first guy who's going to catch bullets from the enemy when they start firing. There were times on patrols when one man would take the point position, and their commander would step up to the front and lead from the front. It's an extremely dangerous, extremely risky thing to do, but they would always volunteer. He would put his platoon sergeant in the back so that if he got taken out, his platoon sergeant could take over.

That's what servant leadership is. I won't have you do anything I wouldn't do myself. With that comes the responsibility to assist. A lot of times, wives wash dishes and stuff like that. Men should step up to the plate and say, *I'll help you*. Little things like that show you care about her.

Now thanks be to God who always leads us in triumph in Christ, and through us diffuses the fragrance of His knowledge in every place.—2 Corinthians 2:14

Anytime we face adversity, Christ is right there with us. He doesn't ask us to do anything that He hasn't done Himself. He's right there with us when He does it.

The third point is not to put unrealistic expectations upon your wife. Anytime you put expectations on people, you're setting yourself up for disappointment and unforgiveness. That's all there's to it. People will never perform at the level of your expectations because I can't fully communicate everything that I expect.

If you're going to do that, get a sheet of paper and write down all the expectations you have for your wife. Give her a report card every day on how she measured up to those expectations. Now, who wants to live under that kind of leadership? I know I wouldn't want to. Inherent in servant leadership is not putting unrealistic expectations on people. You'll find out it's a much better relationship if we don't do that.

The last point is to seek to encourage, motivate, and build up your partner. True servant leadership seeks to build motivation and encouragement into a person. Always say comments like, *Thank you. I appreciate that. You're doing great. You're beautiful. That's helpful. I love you.* Your relationship is built every day—you build into that. You lift that other person up, little thing by little bitty thing.

> *Blessed be the God and Father of our Lord Jesus Christ, the Father of mercies and God of all comfort, who comforts us in all our tribulation, that we may be able to comfort those who are in any trouble, with the comfort with which we ourselves are comforted by God.*—2 Corinthians 1:3-4

See what God does in the midst of trial and tribulation—God lifts us up. He gives us the strength to go forward. The Bible says *the joy of the Lord is my strength* (Nehemiah 8:10). God builds into our lives the strength and encouragement we need, even when we fail. We can't get discouraged with God, because when we come to Him and we confess, He restores us. How could you ever not want to follow a God like that? David said, ' . . . *let me fall into the hands of God for judgment and not into the hands of man. Because God is merciful and gracious toward us*' (2 Samuel 24:14).

God deals with us in love. As husbands, we are to lead in a servant style of leadership. We need to seek to encourage and build up our wife and not tear her down. We need to live with her with an understanding of her needs, not requiring her to do things we wouldn't do. Don't put unrealistic expectations on your wife, and build up and encourage your wife on a daily basis. Marriage is a job. Marriage is a ministry. In a marriage relationship, the husband ministers to his wife, and the wife ministers to her husband. That's how the relationship thrives. And the key to that is forgiveness.

You can't live, and you can't thrive in a relationship with two selfish people where both of them want to control the other. Apart from God, I have nothing good that dwells within me. And so, to whatever degree I submit to God, that is the degree to which I can produce good in my life because it is God producing it through me. The Christian life is not about trying; it's about dying. It's about dying to selfish desires and what I want, submitting those desires to God, and fulfilling the will of God.

We do it to honor and bring glory to God. That's the first lesson on husbands loving your wives. And though God's instruction may be painful, God's instruction produces the fruit of righteousness when we're obedient.

CHAPTER 10

As Christ Loves the Church

How Husbands Love and Lead

What does it look like for a husband to love his wife like Christ loves the Church? It means to be sacrificial in your love towards one another, putting others first; instead of ruling over the wife, serve the wife, and minister to the wife.

As we discussed in the last chapter, there are five major components involved in how a man loves his wife. The first one we looked at in the last chapter is the husband who loves his wife through servant leadership.

The second one we're going to look at in this chapter is presence. A man, in order to love his wife, must have presence in the relationship. Throughout these next chapters, we'll look at the other three aspects: provider, protector, and a promise of good.

When I talk about a husband having presence, what do I mean? You could define the word *presence* as the fact of being or existing, meaning that when someone exists, they have presence. The second definition is that presence means you are visibly present in a place.

A third usage of the word means the way in which one carries them-selves and their bearing. A person can walk into a room, and you say that person has presence. They affect the atmosphere of the room.

But there's another type of presence. The fourth way presence is used is in a spiritual sense. You could say there's a spiritual presence in the room or an evil presence in the room. You come into a church service, and people make comments like, I really sense the presence of the Lord in that place, or I believe God was in on that.

I'm using presence in that the husband, the man in the marriage, should have influence on how the family views life and their respon-sibility before God. That's what a man should be. A man should do that because a man is equipped to be a leader, and men need to be leaders. God's plan for marriage is that marriage resembles Christ and the Church.

How does Christ establish presence in the Church? How can we as men follow that?

The Church's submission to Christ resembles how the Scrip-ture talks about the wife submitting to the husband. And the idea of submission, as previously mentioned, is that the wife respects the husband's position. We, likewise, respect Christ's position in the Church.

But the Church does not submit to Christ in a slave-like form. The Church does not submit to Christ because Christ forces the Church to submit. The Church submits to Christ freely and joy-fully, with a clear understanding of what He desires. So, in a marriage relationship, for the wife to submit to the husband, her submission to the husband should be free and joyful, with a clear understand-ing of what is desired. Christ clearly communicates to the Church, and the Church obeys. And Christ clearly defines how the Church should function and operate. Men are not put into a position of leadership in the home because they're smarter than women. Man is not put in leadership of the home because they are more spiritual than women.

Spiritually, a woman is on the same level as a man. She gets insight from God. She gets guidance from God. She's responsible for her relationship with God. She's getting everything the man's getting. But man is supposed to be in a position of leadership because God's design is for the husband and wife to be together as a united team, bringing up children in the nurture and admonition of the lord.

If you don't have children, then your responsibility is to model what a relationship between two people should look like—like Christ with the Church. Wives should be understanding, joyful, they should express their wisdom, and they should have freedom in the relationship.

Jesus said He would not leave us. Jesus said that He would be there. And what does that mean for us?

My sheep hear My voice, and I know them, and they follow Me. And I give them eternal life, and they shall never perish; neither shall anyone snatch them out of My hand. My Father, who has given them to Me, is greater than all; and no one is able to snatch them out of My Father's hand. I and My Father are one.—John 10:27-30

What does that tell you about Jesus? It tells you and me that we have security in our relationship with Jesus Christ. He's not going to leave us. The Bible tells us Jesus will never leave us nor forsake us. That brings assurance to us in the spiritual life. I can mess up, and I know that Jesus is not going to leave me. I know that Jesus is not going to dump me on the side; He's going to be with me. He's going to be present with me at all times.

A husband should do the same thing in a home. He should be such a point of stability in the relationship that he is not moving. He's not leaving.

Second, in this same chapter, Jesus helps the Church submit for this reason. He's sacrificial in his relationship toward us.

> *I am the good shepherd; and I know My sheep, and am known by My own. As the Father knows Me, even so I know the Father; and I lay down My life for the sheep. And other sheep I have which are not of this fold; them also I must bring, and they will hear My voice; and there will be one flock and one shepherd.*—John 10:14-16

This gives us great confidence that God, the Creator of heaven and earth, is sacrificing Himself on my behalf. There is no greater love than to lay down one's life for His friends, according to what the Scripture tells us in John 3. A husband should likewise be sacrificial in his relationship with his wife and family.

The third point is that the wife should be able to approach the husband whenever she fails or falls short.

> *Seeing then that we have a great High Priest who has passed through the heavens, Jesus the Son of God, let us hold fast our confession. For we do not have a High Priest who cannot sympathize with our weaknesses, but was in all points tempted as we are, yet without sin. Let us therefore come boldly to the throne of grace, that we may obtain mercy and find grace to help in time of need.*—Hebrews 4:14-16

When we come before the Lord when we have failed, the Lord doesn't club us over the head. He treats us with grace. He treats us with mercy. He treats us with kindness. In a relationship, the husband should be the same way when his wife fails, when she falls short, and she comes to that husband; she ought to be treated with grace.

She should not be beaten down by his words. She should not be beaten down emotionally. She should not be taken advantage of or have her failure used as an exploitation to shame and belittle, because God doesn't do that to us. I fail all the time in my walk with God. And you do too. We come before God, and we fail, and we say *God, forgive us,* and what does God do? He blesses us. That's a practical example of how a husband should treat his wife. You should be quick to forgive. You should seek to build them back up, understanding your own shortcomings.

Imperfection Leads Imperfection to Perfection

The Church submits to Christ joyfully, because Christ clearly defines who He is and what He expects. What we have in our relationship with Christ is that as a man, we have imperfection following perfection. My wife is imperfect. She's a sinner. I'm imperfect. I'm a sinner. My Lord is perfect. So you have imperfection following perfection, leading imperfection, to perfection.

The wife is following the Lord, the husband is following the Lord, and yet the husband is also put in a position where he is to lead in that relationship. So how does imperfection (the husband) lead imperfection (the wife) to perfection? Two critical things: humility and integrity. A husband must be a person of humility and integrity. What is integrity? Integrity is doing what is morally upright and proper at all times. Do you know what that does in a relationship? It builds trust in a relationship. If you're a man of integrity, your wife will trust you. Your wife will count what you say as being accurate and upright.

Psalm 25:21 and Proverbs 10:9 both address this issue: how a man who walks with integrity walks securely.

Let integrity and uprightness preserve me, for I wait for You.— Psalm 25:21

He who walks with integrity walks securely, but he who perverts his ways will become known.—(Proverbs 10:9)

He's confident and has assurance. He's not like a piece of Swiss cheese. He doesn't have holes all shot through him. He's solid. *But he who perverts his way will become known* (Proverbs 10:9). In other words, if you lack integrity, it's going to surface eventually. Your lack of integrity will be exposed. Proverbs 11:3 tells us the integrity of the upright will guide them, but the perversity of the unfaithful will destroy them.

We see this in many other places, like Proverbs 20:7 and Proverbs 28:6. But what it all boils down to is that character is more important than material things. Character is the most important thing that we have.

When I was growing up, my father always told me I had to understand that my character means more than anything else that I do. If I don't have character, whatever else I do in life means very little. We have to be honest. We have to be straightforward. We have to be keepers of our word. People have to be able to trust us. Integrity is important, as is humility. The way imperfection leads imperfection to perfection is through humility. Husbands can never think that they're infallible because they're put in a position of leadership. That is called arrogant. That's not Christlike love. Husbands should never think that their wife is less, or that she is less spiritual. She has the same Holy Spirit you have. She has the same Lord that you have. Husbands should not lead in a childish, bullying, one-sided way.

It doesn't matter that he's the breadwinner; it's not his way or the highway. That works great with the world because that's the world's view—an old-fashioned perspective of how a man should be. That's culture. Don't let culture run your life. Run your life in accordance with Scripture. The Bible tells us to operate with humility and meekness. What is meekness? It is not weakness. Meekness is power under control. The most common illustration used for meekness is a horse with a bridle. A horse is a dangerous animal.

One of my jobs when I worked in the prison system was to work with livestock. I was dealing with the horse program, and we had eight stallions out there and about 96 mares. And if you're not careful around a stallion, they will kill you. Plain and simple, they are a vicious and powerful animal, but we knew how to control those animals. They were much stronger than us, but we knew how to control them. That's what meekness is. A horse is meek when it's properly trained. He hasn't lost any power. A man who is meek is a man who has power under control. He has the capacity and the ability to do a lot of things, but he brings it down, and he holds it in check. That's what meekness is. Humility is how we should live. Humility is how we should execute our lives.

At that time Jesus answered and said, "I thank You, Father, Lord of heaven and earth, that You have hidden these things from the wise and prudent and have revealed them to babes. Even so, Father, for so it seemed good in Your sight. All things have been delivered to Me by My Father, and no one knows the Son except the Father. Nor does anyone know the Father except the Son, and the one to whom the Son wills to reveal Him.—Matthew 11:25-27

This is a picture of meekness and humility. This passage clearly defines the fact that Jesus Christ is the ruler of all creation. He sustains not just planet Earth where we are, but the entire systems that exist.

Everything lives and moves and hazards being within him. You can never have that much power. And look how He responds after saying that. *Come to me, all you who labor and are heavy laden, and I will give you rest. Take my yoke upon you and learn from me. For I am gentle and lowly in heart, and you will find rest for your soul, for my yoke is easy and my burden is light,* (Matthew 28-30).

That's power under control. That is power brought under control.

Humility in the Marriage

What about humility? We looked at that in Philippians 2, talking about selfish ambition and conceit and how we are to look out for the interests of others. We are to have a humble mind. A humble mind seeks the well-being of others before itself. That means you put your wife and your children before yourself, that you're willing to sacrifice for their well-being. But it also means that you live your life in such a way that you know where you are and that you are fallible. Don't ever think you're in a position where you can't fail. To be a leader and to be effective in that position, you have to walk with the humility of mind and put the pride behind you.

How does a husband love his wife? By demonstrating a responsibility to God in everything.

As a man, you have to decide the headship of your life. Is it culture? Is it acceptance by other people? Is it money? What defines me as a Christian man? What defines me is my responsibility to God. Why should that define me? Because God is holding us accountable.

For it is written:
As I live, says the Lord, Every knee shall bow to Me, And every tongue shall confess to God. So then each of us shall give account of Himself to God.—Romans 14:11-12

We're going to be accountable for what we do with our life that God has given us.

Therefore, we make it our aim, whether present or absent, to be well pleasing to Him. For we must all appear before the judgment seat of Christ, that each one may receive the things done in the body, according to what He has done, whether good or bad.— 2 Corinthians 5:9-10

That's accountability for what I do with the life God's given me. God gave me a new heart and a new mind, and my sins were forgiven. But God also gave me a new life, and from that day forward until God calls me in His presence, be that through death or if the Lord comes back, I'm accountable for what I do in life. It is no longer my life; it is His life. He gave me this life to live.

He gave me clear instructions on how to live it. If I waste that life by living for self, then I'm going to lose whatever benefit there is in it. What does it profit a man if he gains the whole world and loses his life? What is a profit to a man if he gets everything that there is, and he wastes his life with God? It's of no profit.

They will give an account to Him who is ready to judge the living and the dead.—1 Peter 4:5

All through Scripture, God tells us over and over and over again that we are accountable. In Matthew 16, Jesus asked the question, *Who do people say I am?*

His disciples shared some of the confused theories, so He asked what they thought. Who did they think He was? The answer? "You're the Christ, the son of the living God."

Jesus knew who He was, but He wanted to know who the people thought He was. People who are outside your family have an idea of who you are, but more importantly, your family knows who you are. That's called accountability. That's called home accountability. You're a leader in the home, and you should ask your family, "Who do you say I am?" How does your family define you? Jesus was clearly defined because He was transparent. John 14:6 tells us that He defined Himself as the way, the truth, and the life. He clearly defined who He was, and His disciples knew him.

As leaders, we must clearly define who we are, that we have a responsibility to lead others, and that we have a responsibility to God. Husbands must take the spiritual initiative in the home. Women should never have to prod, plead, or coax their husband to do what is spiritually right and proper in a home. The husband should take that mantle and lead in that direction. A husband should never have to be asked to define *what our plan is, what our purpose is.* They should never have to be asked to address issues in the home. The husband should take the initiative to do that because the husband is responsible to God.

Don't let the woman do that when it's your responsibility to do it. You should be the one who sets the spiritual temperature in the family. The man sets the spiritual temperature in a home, not the woman. Maybe you're thinking, "Well, you don't realize. I have a lot of responsibility. I have to work, and I have a lot on my mind."

No, you've got to sacrifice. That's the first step. It takes sacrifice to do it. Being a husband, being a father, is not an easy job to do. But you have to model the way to those who are around you. And the way you model is to understand your responsibility before God. When a man understands his responsibility before God, his children are going to learn from that.

I learned long ago that people tend to learn more from what they see than what they're told. So, as a man, we have to be responsible to God.

A Moral Vision

The last point is this: a husband has to have a moral vision for life. It falls in line with responsibility to God. It falls in line with imperfection, following perfection, leading imperfection to perfection. All these things line up.

But what does it mean to have a moral vision? It means that as a father, or as a husband, what do you believe about God? What do you believe about the world? What do you believe about the culture? What do you believe about personal responsibility? And as a father or as a husband, your wife should know clearly what you believe about God, what you believe about the world, what you believe about culture, and what you believe about personal responsibility.

Then you have children who come along later, and those children need to know the same things. The way they know that is because you discuss it with them. You clearly tell them what you believe on these subjects. Don't think they're going to learn it on their own. You must clarify where you stand.

We're in the midst of a culture that is rotting. The culture that we live in is no longer going to help you point your family in the right direction. And this world needs to know where Christian men stand. What do we believe in? What do we think about the world around us? The time of passivity and silence is gone. We must clearly define where we stand, and that begins with our own families. The only way to stop a spinning world is when the Church starts to be the salt and light of the world.

The way you become the salt and light of the world is to focus on your wife and focus on your children. You've got to train them up to where they clearly know the direction to go.

A lot of Christians have no problem putting the rainbow flag symbol on things they have and endorsing the lifestyle that flag represents.

Why would you endorse or give approval to something that grieves the heart of God? These marginal Christians do it because they're more concerned with what other people think about them than what God says.

We should reach out to all people in love, humility, and kindness. What they do in their personal life is their business. But you don't have to support it. You don't have to agree with it.

You must always love your neighbors as yourself. But where do you stand? Do your children know? Men, we've got to be leaders. We've got to stand up. When things are right, do we endorse them? When things are wrong, do we speak out? Do we clearly let our family know? Does our family have a moral vision of what direction they should go? Because as men, we should be doing that with our families. We should be doing that with our children. You have to tell them the truth, and you have to quit being afraid. People are so afraid of what other people say.

The cross of Christ is going to create conflict. That comes with it. Jesus told His disciples to count the cost. Like them, we have to know there's a price to pay. He said that if the world speaks good of you, shame be under you. Stop trying to court the world. Stop trying to court the approval of other people. You're not going to stand and give an account to those people, but you will to God.

We have to clearly decide as individuals, where do I stand? What do I believe in? And as men, we have to communicate that to our wife, and we have to communicate it to our children. We have to make a clear and definitive statement of what is right and wrong.

Part of the problem with our culture today is weak, sissy, passive, men. That is a major problem. I've got two daughters and two sons. My daughter, in conversation, made that comment to me. I never really thought about it, but I got the woman's perspective. I asked what the problem is with men today. She said that the problem with men today is they are wimps. They are sissies, they are passive, they don't care, and they are feminine.

The reason for this is because that's what culture ruled back in the 60s. That culture began to erupt in our society, and men were put in a place where they were viewed as being less than what they should be. A lot of it was because of poor leadership on the part of men. A lot of men are totalitarians—they will slap a woman around, but they won't face a man.

But a true man can stand on his own and is not fearful of what other people think. If you're running around worried about what other people think, you better get your house in order about what God thinks.

You're going to give an account to God one day. Men have to take up the mantle of manhood, but manhood is not running around bossing people around and being a bully. Manhood isn't being over-bearing. Being a man is defined by Scripture. It's leading with love and humility and kindness and gentleness. You don't have to express your manhood outwardly all the time. Seek to glorify God in your life. Change priorities in your life. You may have to get before God now and say, "God, I have not done this. But I am stopping today."

There are people in the Bible that did just that. Joshua 24 shows us an example of a servant leader and warrior who led his men to the promise land with the assurance from God that they would conquer the enemy.

A group of 12 went and they were terrified of the Philistines who looked like giants. They didn't think they stood a chance. But Caleb and Joshua knew God had made them a promise. If they followed His headship, He would lead them to victory.

And because of that? They got rid of the cowards. They wiped out the whole generation of men who didn't trust God and let fear of man rule over them.

In verse 14, He urges the fear of the Lord. He instructs that they should do nothing in life but what is pleasing to the Lord and to serve him in sincerity, integrity, and truth. He tells them to put away the gods that their fathers worshiped back in Egypt.

To many these days, it seems evil to ask men to turn their backs on the culture of their fathers. If it seems evil to you, these are people that God has led in victory, but they've defected. They've gone back to the enemies of God. God, through Joshua, asked the question, "Does it seem evil to you to serve the Lord?"

We have to ask ourselves today. Am I going to serve culture, opinion, and popularity? What am I going to serve in my life? If it seems evil to you to serve the Lord, choose for yourself this day, who you will serve? God is saying that either you get in or get out. As for me and my house, we will serve the Lord. Every one of us as men have to make that call. We have to decide if we're going to serve the gods of culture, compromise, the gods of passivity, of human acceptance, or if we're going to serve the true and living God. The true and living God will bring blessings and abundance to your life and to the lives of your wife and to your children. God works through solid leadership.

As men, each one of us must make that decision. Who are you going to serve this day? Have you made that call clear with your wife? Have you made that call clear with your family? Whether you realize that or not, we are in a cultural war and as parents, as families, as husbands, as men, we must train up the generation coming after us. We must be willing to be a voice of clarity and a voice of truth, guided by compassion, love, and humility for others. We owe it to our children. We owe it to our wife. We owe it to our friends. But it's going to take each one of us taking up that call. It's not done through rudeness or pride, but through humility and love. Love your wife as Christ loved the Church.

Do you have a presence in your home? Does your family know what we believe and where we stand on all these issues? We must have presence. Christ has presence in the Church. We must have presence in our family. Put your past behind you, repent, turn from that path, and put your focus on God. It's a decision we make all the time. We have to constantly check ourselves. And we have to live in the presence of a merciful God.

CHAPTER 11

The Provider

How does a Husband Provide
for His Family?

In this chapter, we're going to focus on provision. We're going to see how, in loving their wives as Christ loved the Church, husbands love them by providing for them.

What does it mean to provide? What is provision? What does that mean? Provision is the act of providing or supplying something of need. So, the husband has a responsibility to provide for the needs of the family. The first provision that the husband makes is what I call the provision of position. The provision of position is when the husband loves the wife. Again, the word that's used about the relationship with the wife is the word *agape*.

The husband loves the wife because of her position in the relationship, not her performance in the relationship. Love for the wife is not based upon what she does. It's based upon a sacrificial act of the will that the husband loves his wife, even when the wife comes short. With that comes the responsibility that our love for our wife must be there even when the wife fails or falls short.

We know this because I fall short in my relationship with God all the time, and yet God's love for me doesn't change. God's love for me is not built upon what I do. His love for me is not built upon how faithful I am, or how consistent I am, or how obediently I act. His love for me is based upon the fact that I am in Christ Jesus, and I'm in a relationship with him. So the husband is to love his wife in the same way. He loves his wife because his wife is in the position of his help-meet in the relationship. She is his completer.

Colossians 2 reminds us that we were dead in our trespasses but have been made alive in Christ since He has forgiven us for all of our trespasses. In verse 13, we are urged to bear with one another and forgive others as Christ forgave us.

A husband in relationship with his wife must have a forgiving heart towards his wife, just like God is forgiving towards us. Just as Christ has forgiven us, so we must forgive them. 1 John 1:9 reminds us that if we confess, we are forgiven. A very important part of a marriage relationship is forgiveness towards one another. You've got to be able to forgive each other and let things go.

What causes us not to forgive? Our own selfishness. We think we are above what we receive, or we put unrealistic expectations on another person, and when they don't treat us the way we think they should treat us, we hold them in debt for that. When it comes to forgiveness, you have to think less of yourself and more of that other person. Think of yourself in relationship to God, and what does God do on your behalf when you fail? God forgives.

Physical Provision

The second aspect here is physical provision. The first one is positional provision, but the second one is physical provision. Physical provision means providing physical sustenance for life.

What does that revolve around? Primarily food and shelter. It is the husband's responsibility to provide for the family. Remember, you don't *have* to get married. Some people spend their lives single, and that's perfectly fine. But if you choose to get married, when you, as a man, make a choice to marry, you've taken on additional responsibility. I think a lot of people fail to understand that. They still have a selfish mindset. They still want themselves first. But when you get married, as a man, you've taken on further responsibility in your life. And with that further responsibility comes the need to provide food and shelter for the wife.

> *For you yourselves know how you ought to follow us, for we were not disorderly among you; nor did we eat anyone's bread free of charge, but worked with labor and toil night and day, that we might not be a burden to any of you, not because we do not have authority, but to make ourselves an example of how you should follow us. For even when we were with you, we commanded you this: If anyone will not work, neither shall he eat. For we hear that there are some who walk among you in a disorderly manner, not working at all, but are busybodies. Now those who are such we command and exhort through our Lord Jesus Christ that they work in quietness and eat their own bread.*—2 Thessalonians 3:7-12

Work is God's means of provision for us. It's very important for husbands to understand that it is their responsibility as the husband to provide for the physical needs of their wife.

1 Peter 5:7 reminds us to cast all our cares on Christ, for He cares for us. If husbands love their wives as Christ loves the Church, then they have to care for the needs of the wife.

Philippians 4:19 says, *God will supply all of our needs according to His riches and glory by Christ Jesus.* God provides for our needs. That is a responsibility on us as men to do that in the family. There's nothing wrong with a woman working outside the home, but if a woman works outside the home, the man is still responsible for the needs of the home. And if the woman works outside the home, then the husband must understand that some of the responsibilities within the home need to be shared. A lot of men have wives who work outside the home, and when the wife comes home, the man just plops down. He doesn't do anything. He expects the women to get in the kitchen and make him some supper and clean the house. Your wife is not designed to have two jobs. And if she's going to have her primary focus outside the house, then when it comes to within the house, there should be some shared duties and responsibility.

But even if your wife doesn't work outside the house, there still should be some shared duties and responsibilities in a home, even if the sharing is to the extent of you just picking up after yourself. Throwing stuff around and expecting your wife to be a housemaid and go behind you and clean up that's disrespectful and not honoring to your wife. If your wife is the queen of the home, you treat her like the queen of the home. Be willing to help in those areas. If you see something in the house that needs to be cleaned up, clean it up. It's not that big of a deal.

In marriage, people tend to get siloed, and they think *that's not my responsibility to do that. It's her responsibility.* But it's a shared responsibility. In order for a home to function, you've got to look at it as a shared responsibility.

Another way you provide for your wife is not to take foolish financial risks with the money in the home. Too often, men start throwing their money into depreciating assets that don't grow in value. You have to learn to control your spending in those areas. Because as you spend money on depreciating assets, you're taking resources away that could be used for other areas in the home. So it has to be done with a cooperative mindset. I hear men all the time saying, "I'm the bread-winner in the home; I spend my money on what I want to."

When you take someone else into your home, you have a shared responsibility in that area. You could put your family in great financial risk by being foolish with your money. You need to be a wise steward of the money you have.

We can see that providing for your wife physically is more than just food and shelter. It's meeting the needs that she has, and it's a system with responsibilities around the home and providing sound financial direction for the home. If you don't know how to do that, there are a lot of resources out there. Dave Ramsey is an excellent resource, as well as Larry Burkett. There are a lot of excellent resources for finances. But if you're on a limited income, then you have to be on a limited expenditure.

Think about it like this: when you start out, you don't have much. It takes time, but over time, you accumulate stuff. But people, because of our selfish mindset, we try to go out and grab everything right at the front, and when you do, it's going to put your family in a financial risk. That leads to anxiety and worry, which impacts the emotions in the home.

Emotional Provision

The third area of provision is emotional provision.

God blesses and loves the Church by guiding us through life. And a husband should be there to help guide the wife. You provide by guiding. God is our great shepherd, according to the Scripture. Psalm 23 says, *The Lord is my shepherd, I shall not want.* I shall not want is better translated from Hebrew as *The Lord is my shepherd, I will lack nothing.*

God provides for everything we have, not just physically, but He also provides for us emotionally. He guides us in life. He is our light. He is the one who leads us.

Psalm 48:14 is a small verse that reminds us He is God, our God forever and ever, and He will be our guide even to death. God guides us, and that's a sign of God's law for us. Therefore, as husbands, we should guide in the home. What is a good way we can guide in the home? One of the good ways we can guide in the home is by being an encourager for the wife. Proverbs 12:25 teaches us, ". . . anxiety in the heart of man causes depression, but a good word makes it glad." If a husband is an encourager in a home, and he brings a good word, he will create a positive attitude and influence in the home.

That's extremely important—to be positive. If you're tired or grouchy when you come home from work, you can change the entire tone in the house. Another thing is that the Bible tells us in 1 Peter 3:7 to dwell with our wives with understanding. That means as a husband, you need to understand your wife. Women are very different than men. Very different.

Men will confront one another head-on. But I'll say something to my wife, I look over, and she'll have her hand on her hip or something, looking at me, clearly upset.

Men are dumb when it comes to that kind of stuff. A wife will say, "I don't appreciate what you said." Confused, the man will ask, "What did I say? I didn't say anything wrong." "It's the way you said it," she'll reply. I know if you're married, you've heard your wife say that at least once in your married life.

That's something I learned when I got married. It's not what you say. It can be the way you say it. I came in one day, and my wife asked what I was mad about. I said, "I'm not mad about anything." She said, "Well, you look mad." The cycle of discussion continued, so I tried to show a happier face, given that I really wasn't mad about anything.

I didn't understand what about me gave that impression, but if that bothers her, it's incumbent upon me to change it.

As tough as that is for guys, if you want to dwell with your wife, you've got to learn to alter not just what you say and not just what you do, but how you do it. I remember as a kid getting a few whippings from my dad. I'd have to get a "tune-up," as he called it, about every four or five years, and he'd light my world up again. I'd be back on the right track and go in the right direction. But one of the things he often pointed out was, "It's not what you're doing, son. It's your attitude when you do it."

Though I might be sitting down, I'd be standing up on the inside. He could detect a negative attitude in me that quickly. The same thing is true in a marriage relationship. Women are more emotionally driven. Things that bother a woman don't bother a man. You start taking risks in your marriage, doing foolish things, quitting this job, starting this job without communicating with your wife, and that makes a woman nervous and unsteady. Women want a stable, positive home life.

You have to understand that the home, just like with birds, is a woman's nest. You go messing with her nest, and she's going to swell up on you. If you go in there and mess with a hen that's sitting on some eggs, it doesn't end well. Your wife will do the same thing. When she does that, you're in trouble. You'd better get your hand away from the nest, and you'd better figure out what to do to fix it. It all has to do with the emotional provision. It's providing for the emotional needs of women. You can wreck a marriage just by damaging a woman emotionally because they view that as very similar to physical abuse.

It's very important for men to create a stable home. So, when your wife is criticizing your tone, and it frustrates you, you have to be sensitive. I don't mean sensitive like the world thinks of sensitive men. I'm talking about having ears to hear. Be perceptive, be alert, and be vigilant in the way you go about your life. Understand that selfishness says, "I don't care how you feel. I don't care. I didn't say anything bad. I didn't do anything bad." But if it's perceived that way, then you did. And you have to deal with that.

Spiritual Provision

Finally, the last area after emotional provision is spiritual provision. Positional provision is showing love. Physical provision is providing for the needs and caring for the wife. Emotional provision is administering to her emotional aspects. Spiritual provision can be seen in a lot of ways, but one of the most important ways it's seen is the example of how Christ intercedes for us.

As men, we need to be interceding for our wives. A husband should pray daily for his wife. It's very, very important that you pray daily for your wife.

Confess your trespasses to one another and pray for one another that you may be healed. The effective fervent prayer of a righteous man avails much.—James 5:16

If you're going to be a righteous man, a spiritual leader in the home, you've got to learn how to pray for your wife, and for your children as well, if you have any. Pray for their protection. Pray for their physical health, and pray for them to be shielded from the presence of evil. Pray that they'd be grounded spiritually. Pray that they'd be brought into favor with those they come into contact with. That's intercessory prayer, and it's our responsibility as men, as spiritual leaders.

Therefore, submit to God. Resist the devil, then he will flee from you.—James 4:7

How do you resist the devil? Prayer. Don't just pray for yourself, pray for your family, pray for the needs of your home. Pray for the needs of your children, pray for the well-being of your children. Pray that they'd be granted guidance and protection. A lot of times, I pray for my wife as I'm leaving home. Sometimes, as I leave, God will bring to my attention that we didn't leave on a good note. Maybe I left with a rotten attitude that morning.

At times, I've stopped my vehicle and turned around and come home or picked up a phone to call her and apologize, because I know I was wrong. If you pray for your wife, God will show you many times where you're messing up in your life. You just have to be willing to fix the things you do wrong. And if you love your wife as Christ loved the Church, that's exactly what you will do. You may be hard-headed, and God may have to tap your drum a few times, but when you sense the Holy Spirit prompting you about something, you need to deal with it. You need to listen when the Holy Spirit shows you when you're wrong because you need to be praying for your family. I cannot stress that enough.

Pray for your wife and children. God uses that many times to help you become sensitive to the needs that are there. Prayer is a powerful tool in a marriage relationship. Pray for their emotional, physical, and spiritual well-being. Intercede, just like God intercedes for you, and God intercedes for me. Prayer is a powerful tool.

When George McCluskey started a family, he decided that he would invest one hour every day in prayer because he wanted his children to follow Christ. Then he expanded his prayers to include his grandchildren and his great-grandchildren. Every day between 11 a.m. and noon, he prayed for the next three generations of his life. As the years went by, his two daughters both committed their lives to Christ and married men who went into ministry. These two couples produced four girls and one boy. Each of the girls from those relationships married a minister, and the boy became a pastor. The first two children born to this generation were boys. After leaving secondary school, the two cousins, these two boys, chose the same college and became roommates.

During their second year, one boy decided to go into the ministry. The other didn't. He felt lots of pressure to continue the family legacy, but he chose to go a different pathway. He chose instead to go his own way and pursue his interest in psychology. He earned his doctorate and eventually wrote books for parents that became best-sellers. Eventually, he started a radio program that was heard around the world every day. The man's name is James Dobson. So, now you know the story of George McCluskey. He was just an ordinary man, but his prayers had an extraordinary effect on much of the world.

If you are a parent or a grandparent, the word for you today is to arise, cry out in the night, pour out your heart like water before the face of the Lord, lift your hands toward Him for the life of your children, and your wife, and your family in general. As men, you need to pray for your wife, you need to pray for your children, and you need to pray for God's will and blessing upon them. Pray also that God grants you wisdom, and what to do, and how to do it. Providing for the wife is a demonstration of love. It's an act of love in a relationship, providing for the needs, but the needs go beyond just physical things. The needs go into the spiritual realm, the needs go into love, the needs go into the emotional realm. It's a 360° circle where all these areas are met, and that's what true provision in the family is.

CHAPTER 12
Protecting the Wife
A Husband's Duty for Protection in the Home

The books of Galatians, Ephesians, Philippians, and Colossians are collectively referred to as the Prison Epistles. Paul wrote these letters to different churches while in prison, and they're very similar. The passage we looked at in Ephesians 5 is more of an expansion upon what we're focusing on in Colossians 3:19. Colossians 3:19 tells husbands to love their wives and not be bitter towards them.

I can write a book on the topic of husbands, love your wife, but the thing that would pop into your mind is, what does that mean to love your wife? When you go to the passage in Ephesians, it says, *Husbands, love your wives as Christ loved the Church* (Ephesians 5:25). That gives us a little more insight into the life of Christ and how Christ relates to the Church.

We're now going to look at protection and what it means for a husband to protect his wife. Protection is just another facet of love. We'll see how that's played out with Christ and the Church, and then with a husband and the wife.

How does Christ protect the Church? John 10:11 tells us how He laid down His life for the sheep. He sacrifices for us, but through that, He is also providing us protection because through His death, He ensures for us eternal life when we trust in him.

> *Jesus answered, "I have told you that I am He. Therefore, if you seek Me, let these go their way," that the saying might be fulfilled which He spoke, "Of those whom You gave Me I have lost none.—John 18:8-9*

By keeping His sheep, we see a demonstration of love on behalf of Christ, because He keeps His own. In Hebrews 13:5, He says He will never leave you nor forsake you. All those statements that Christ makes are different facets of His love for the Church. He loves the Church, and He protects the Church, because we are humans. We have a tendency to move away from God, not towards God. It's through the power of God that He's able to keep us. He draws us back into right relationships with Him. He moves on us when we get out of line, and it's because of His love. He told His disciples He would build His Church, and He said the gates of hell will not prevail against it. He is a protector.

If Christ is a protector, then husbands should be protectors. 1 Peter 3 says, *Husbands should dwell with the wife with understanding, giving honor to the wife as to the weaker vessel, being heirs together with the grace of life, that their prayers may not be hindered.*

Women are physically weaker than men--it's just the way women are made. Now, some women are strong and aggressive, but by and large, men do dominate women. Even in our culture, where we see the equality of men and women, the Bible also speaks of the equality of men and women. Women are spiritually equal to men in their relationship with God. They're just as accountable to God as the men are. So, when we talk about women as the weaker vessel, it's just a construct of how women are physically.

Therefore, in the marital team, men are put in a position of protector. Even with the proclamations of equality in our culture, women and children are preyed upon across the globe. In our culture, people still take advantage of them. And so, it's inherent upon the man, if he loves his wife, to also protect his wife. How does a man protect his wife? He protects his wife physically.

There are elements within our culture that seek to prey upon weakness. Men have to be vigilant to guard and protect against that. If you notice something about predatory animals in the wild, like lions, for example, they prey on the weaker ones in the herd. They prey on the young and the weak. I saw a clip where a zebra got into the water and a crocodile got ahold of the zebra. He was wearing that zebra out and had him by the leg, and the zebra fought, and fought, and fought. Finally, he got loose. His leg was messed up, likely broken. He came up the side of the little river, and all the other zebras were all happy because he made it. Well, there's a lion there, and the lion jumps out, gets him by the throat, takes him to the ground, and kills him. That's the function of the zebra. The function of a zebra or an antelope in Africa is to feed the lion—that's its role.

I know people pull for the underdog, but why is a zebra's life more important than a lion's? That lion has to eat; that zebra is there to provide food for the lion. But the characteristic I want you to look at is how they identify the weak in the group. Human beings, in their fallen nature, are constructed in a very similar manner. Human beings will prey upon the weak also. There are people in our society and in our culture who are seeking an opportunity to prey upon your family, to get your wife, and to get your children, and that's just the reality of the world we live in today.

So, a husband has a role to protect his wife. Inherent in that is to protect his children too. He protects his wife physically, but also by not putting her in a dangerous place to live. Make sure your home is a safe place, and make sure your wife feels safe in that home and protected in that home. You have to protect your wife against other men. Be cautious with other men involving themselves in a relationship with your wife. By relationship, what I mean is communicating with your wife or without other people being around. Women are more drawn to communication than men are.

When you engage in conversations with women or other men engage in conversations with your wife, you have to be very cautious. It's not that you're some kind of control freak, but be alert as to what's going on. Be alert as far as the arena of salespeople, scam artists, and people like that. They will prey on the emotional aspect many times.

Most women are pretty astute to that; some of them are more astute than a man, but it happens all the time. That's why the door-to-door salesman, a lot of times, will just talk to the wife. My wife and I had been married a couple of years when we were buying a car. I was driving a hard deal, and my wife spoke up in the middle of the debate between me and the car salesman, and she reminded me that he had to feed his family too. I told her to let me handle it. We got out of there, and I said, "In the future, don't take his side like that." She said she felt sorry for him, and I was being so hard on him. A lot of times, salespeople know that, and they will exploit that.

Spiritual Protection

So, you have to protect your wife in the physical sense. But I think there's an area that's much more important than the physical protection, and that is spiritual protection of the wife. How does a man spiritually protect his wife? In order for a man to spiritually protect his wife, you've got to take care of yourself first.

If you've ever flown, you've likely listened to the safety briefing from the flight attendant. They explain what to do in case of an emergency, like a rapid descent or sudden loss of cabin pressure. One thing they mention is that if oxygen levels drop, an oxygen mask will drop down from the ceiling in front of you. They always remind you to put your own mask on first, before helping others—whether that's a child or someone who needs assistance. You've probably heard that part before.

There's a reason for that. In order to help that child or help that other person, you have to make sure you're able to breathe. Once you put your mask on, you can help deal with the needs of the other people on that plane. The same thing is true in the spiritual arena. If a man is going to protect his wife spiritually, he needs to make sure his spiritual life is in order first.

Take care of yourself first. As a man, are you spending time in prayer? Are you regularly reading the Word of God? It's crucial to intake Scripture, whether by reading it or listening to it, even while driving. This helps fill your mind with God's truth and keeps you focused on Him. Another important area to address is consistency in your walk with God—both at home and outside of it. You can't live a dual life, pretending to be spiritual only on Sunday mornings or in front of your family, while acting differently at work or elsewhere. Spiritual consistency is key, and it's something you must live out in every part of your life.

You have to have consistency in your work. That means it's going to cost you to live like this, but the Bible has no room for a dual life. A short word for that is hypocrisy, which comes from the Greek word hypokrite. A hypocrite in the Greek world was an actor. It meant that they played a part. Don't be a hypocrite when it comes to the faith. Don't just play like you're a spiritual person, be a spiritual person, be a spiritual man. And in order to be a spiritual man, you're going to have to put your mask on first. You're going to have to make sure that you get your spiritual house in order and that you're in fellowship with God.

Spiritual discernment is the ability to look beyond what you see on the surface and realize there is a spiritual reality to the world we live in. Many men are, for lack of a better phrase, tone-deaf or punch-drunk, spiritually unaware of the world around them.

There are a lot of men in the spiritual arena who don't discern spiritual things very quickly. You've got to be spiritually alert to what's going on because there are spiritual forces in the world that are after not just your wife but your children, too. And if you're going to be a true leader, then you've got to be spiritually strong. You've got to put your oxygen mask on first and make sure you get your personal house in order to serve others spiritually.

In the early chapters, we looked through Genesis 3 and the fall of man in the garden. In the midst of that story, we are introduced to the serpent, who was cunning and twisted God's Words for his own deceitful purposes.

Who was the command given to concerning that tree? It was given to Adam. When the serpent comes into the picture, the deceiver knows exactly what to do. He goes to the woman. But consider the verse at the very end. It says she also gave the fruit to her husband, who was with her, and he ate. During this whole spiritual temptation, Adam was right there with his wife, and he failed to take the lead. This is before the fall. This is before they were sinful, and I've studied that passage a lot, and I've tried to get some insight into it, but I come away with the same conclusion. There was something inborn in man to be passive on a lot of issues. That's an opinion, but that's what I think. You can come up with your own conclusion by reading the Scripture. But when I look at the Scripture, that's a stunning passage when you realize that Adam was right there the whole time, and he failed to take the lead.

I think it's the work of the evil one, but it's also a work of our flesh. For some reason, we tend to minimize things that are spiritual, and we push that over to the side of the woman to read the Bible and pray with the child. In reality, God has put you as the head of the family. It is your responsibility and my responsibility as a man to take a spiritual lead.

Being the Spiritual Leader

Take care of your own spiritual needs first, but have spiritual discernment for what's going on around you as a man. One of the best gifts you can give to your family as a husband is to have a solid spiritual walk with the Lord. That's one of the best things you can have as a spiritual leader in your family.

What you do speaks louder than what you say. Spiritual leadership is where you take the initiative and lead the family. In a home, that would involve you leading your family in worship. You would make that a priority. You would make God first, your family second, and yourself third. *Seek first the kingdom of God and His righteousness, and all these things will be added unto you,* (Matthew 6:33 ESV). Scripture makes it abundantly clear.

And I understand that as human beings, we're going to fail. We're going to fall short. We do it all the time, but spiritual leadership is consistency over a long period of time, good times and bad times.

What are some practical ways that you can provide spiritual protection and spiritual leadership in the home? Consider what your family listens to in music, what they watch on TV, and what kind of movies they watch. You've got to be discerning of what's going on.

Over the last 20 years, there's been a big rise in the popularity of reality TV. The whole concept of reality TV is a total deception. It's all scripted. So, what does that tell you? They have an agenda. Everything that comes across on a visual screen like that has a purpose and an agenda. They want to draw people to watch it. They want to make money. But if you understand the worldview of most of the people who are in that field, it is not a God-honoring industry. I'm not saying you should be completely separated and never have anything to do with it, but I'm saying you've got to be discerning on what you watch.

You've got to set up standards and guidelines about what is going to be permissible in your home and what your family is exposed to outside the home. As a spiritual leader in a home and as a father, you've got to be alert and aware as to what your children are being taught. Women tend to be more involved in that than men, but don't push that burden over on the wife solely. You have a responsibility as a man to know what's going on. You talk to teachers in a public school. Don't put an undue burden on your wife; that's not loving towards her to have her hold that whole responsibility.

There's a concept here that the school owns your kids and can do with your kids what they want to, but those are your children. Those children don't belong to the school; they belong to you. What is being put in their head is put in there with your permission. If you play like Adam and sit on the sideline and let it happen, there are people who will captivate the mind of your child. According to Proverbs 23, *As a man thinks in his heart, so is he.* You change the thinking of a person; you will change the actions of a person.

That is a common practice that's been carried out since the beginning of mankind.

You have every right to look into what's happening in the schools and investigate. When it comes to your children dating, you should also have a definite say on that. Women are much quicker to pick up where a girl is, and a man is a lot quicker to pick up on where a guy is. It's just a reality. So, know what's going on with the young men and women your children are involved with.

You've got to be a spiritual leader when it comes to the arena of sexual immorality. Sexual immorality covers every sin outside of marriage. Every sex act outside of a man and a woman in marriage is sexual immorality. The Bible condemns sexual immorality. As a father, you need to take on this role; don't put that burden on your wife. You take that role, and you instruct as far as that goes. Another area you need to be alerted to is attitudes and unforgiveness in the home. If you're spiritually alert and you're spiritually discerning, you can tell when someone is struggling with bitterness or unforgiveness, and you need to deal with it. You need to have them sit down, and you need to talk to them.

As a husband and father, many times bad attitudes in the home have been caused by stuff I've done. I'd said things wrong; I'd done things wrong, and it created bitterness or unforgiveness in my children or wife. And you may ask and hear the answer, "I'm fine; it's fine; nothing's wrong." Brother, when you hear that, that means there's a major issue at hand. That's generally a woman telling you that you have messed up.

Once you finally get it out in the open, if you're the cause of the problem, you're going to have to forgive, and you're going to have to ask forgiveness in that relationship. Because if you fail to do that, those attitudes will keep on. Look at Isaac in the Bible. He had two sons, Jacob and Esau. Isaac is in the book of Hebrews Chapter 11 as being a great man of faith. When we look at Isaac, we see the faith of Isaac.

But Isaac was a passive man in his home. He favored one son, Esau, and his wife favored the other son, Jacob, and he allowed that to go on and on. And as a result, it created a major war between those two boys

Every person outside of Jesus Christ has faults, has shortcomings, including the great men of Scripture. That tells me that as a man, I've got faults and shortcomings in my own life. We need to address those issues, and a lot of time, it's going to take you humbling yourself and apologizing to set the record straight. You also have to understand that all your children and your wife are different.

Often, it's not what you say, but how you say it. When conflict arises in a relationship, it's essential to address it—ignoring it or pretending it didn't happen, like Adam did, isn't an option. As the spiritual leader of your home, you need to be proactive in addressing issues, especially those that involve the spiritual health of the family. Even if you're at fault, you must be willing to take responsibility and work toward a resolution. As a man, embracing spiritual leadership means being willing to first get yourself spiritually aligned before you can lead others.

Being the spiritual leader in your home means prioritizing the growth and well-being of everyone around you. It's about pushing others to rise, helping them become better, and being willing to sacrifice your own comfort to make that happen. This is the true essence of headship. When Scripture says, "Love your wife as Christ loved the Church," it's not a call to dominate or control, but to lead through love, humility, and sacrifice. Christ doesn't rule over the Church in a harsh, overbearing way—He leads with grace and for our ultimate good. In the same way, a man is called to lead his family with love, aiming for their spiritual and personal growth.

To truly embody this leadership, a man must be discerning— aware of the needs of his family and spiritually in tune to know how to guide them. Spiritual leadership isn't just a role; it's a responsibility that shapes the health of the entire family. Biblically speaking, the spiritual state of the family directly impacts the physical and emotional well-being of the home. A family that is spiritually grounded will thrive in every other area of life.

Spiritual leaders attune to danger around the family. A spiritual leader is in touch with what's going on with each member of their family, especially their wife, to realize what needs to be done here to make this better, and that's what we've got to do. We fail often, and you will fail, but failure is not final. A man shows his love for his wife by being a spiritual leader in a home. Being a spiritual leader is what our nation needs more than anything. The only thing that is going to turn our nation around is a spiritual awakening. It's inherent upon us as members of the body of Christ to take the lead and set the example, because we live in a dark world, and people need hope. They need to know where to look and get help.

Husbands, love your wives as Christ loved the Church and gave Himself for her (Ephesians 5:25). Jesus loves the Church by protecting the Church. He provides us guidelines, insight, protection, guidance, direction, and more, and that's how a man should be with his wife.

CHAPTER 13
The Promise of Good
How a Husband Brings Goodness into the Home

The man is a leader in a home to promote a positive, good environment within the home. He is supposed to be a motivator, a leader, and able to set the tone in the house. It's very important that husbands understand the importance of their role in that, but we're also going to look at the basic components of marriage, which all lead to a united front. Being a good husband involves everything, like the promise of provision, the promise of faithfulness, the promise of faithfulness to God, and within that, the promise of faithfulness to the wife. It all includes fidelity, acceptance, and forgiveness, and how those play into the overall relationship in the home.

When we talk about the promise of good, this all comes under the headline of husbands loving their wives as Christ loves the Church. When we talk about love and talk about the relationship between Christ and the Church, one of the topics that comes up is that Christ promises good for us.

How is God good? God is good because the character of God is good. That's one of His character traits. God is a good God. Therefore, everything that God does is going to be good. That's why we can say things like *He causes all things to work together for good, for those who love Him and are called according to His purpose* (Romans 8:28 paraphrase). God is a God of good; therefore, what He produces for us is good.

If a husband is to love his wife, as Christ loves the Church, one of the things a husband should do for the wife and for the home is to make a promise for good for the family and to produce good for the family. The first promise for good in a family relationship is the promise of faithfulness.

Now, the promise of faithfulness to God comes first. The man in the home has to promise faithfulness to God in order to be effective with his family. For example, a husband should have a mindset that he will keep himself strong spiritually so he can discern evil and protect his family. That is a basic responsibility of the man in the home.

> *For this reason we also, since the day we heard it, do not cease to pray for you, and to ask that you may be filled with the knowledge of His will in all wisdom and spiritual understanding; that you may walk worthy of the Lord, fully pleasing Him, being fruitful in every good work and increasing in the knowledge of God; strengthened with all might, according to His glorious power, for all patience and longsuffering with joy; giving thanks to the Father who has qualified us to be partakers of the inheritance of the saints in the light.*—Colossians 1:9-12

That's our role in life. We are to live our lives to please God. Therefore, in a marriage relationship, it's very important for the man to prioritize his relationship with God.

One of the problems is that a lot of Christian men, in particular, seem to be somewhat timid about their relationship with Christ. The most important relationship you can possibly have is your relationship with God Almighty.

It's very common to hear, "I believe in God, but I believe that my faith is a private thing. It's a personal thing." When it comes to the Christian faith, the Bible says that our faith is not a private thing. Jesus tells us to let our light shine. He tells us to be salt and to make a difference in the world that we live in. Those are very important things. He tells us to be open and to proclaim His truth, to go into all the world and preach the gospel. A Christian faith should be an open faith. That means that a husband should live and lead by faith. Your house should be a place to serve the lord, a place where God is honored. The home should be a refuge from the world and not a partner of the world. The only way that's going to happen is when the man puts his relationship with God as first and foremost. The second thing outside of a promise of faithfulness to God would be a promise of provision for the family in the sense that you keep the promises that you've made.

You have a promise to be faithful. When you go to a wedding ceremony, the man and the woman in that ceremony, in most cases, exchange vows. One of the very common vows in a marriage relationship is, "I will put you first and foremost in my life. I will stay with you through sickness and through health, through good times and bad times, and all down the line." But a lot of people see vows as more of a ritualistic thing, versus what God sees as a vow.

A vow is a declaration of commitment. When we make a declaration of commitment in a Christian arena, it's not just to the wife or husband. It's not just for the people who are there to witness the ceremony. Ultimately and foremost, it's a commitment to God.

Do not be rash with your mouth,
And let not your heart utter anything hastily before God.
For God is in heaven, and you on earth;
Therefore, let your words be few.
For a dream comes through much activity,
And a fool's voice is known by his many words.
When you make a vow to God, do not delay to pay it;
For He has no pleasure in fools.
Pay what you have vowed—
Better not to vow than to vow and not pay.—Ecclesiastes 5:2-5

God holds us accountable for these vows. Therefore, you have to remain faithful to them. One of the reasons it's so important is that God is faithful.

God is faithful, by whom you are called in the fellowship of His Son, Jesus Christ, our Lord.—1 Corinthians 1:9

Let us hold fast the confession of our hope without wavering, for He who promised is faithful.—Hebrews 10:23

God is faithful to keep His Word. And as men, we have to be faithful to keep our word. So, how is faithfulness seen in a marriage relationship in a Christian marriage?

Fidelity

Fidelity in a relationship means to stay true to the one you are married to. That's extremely important. Put your wife first. Outside of your relationship with God, your most important relationship is a relationship with your wife. You have to cultivate that relationship.

First, don't compare your wife to other women. Most women do not like that. That seems like a little thing, but when marriages break up, they usually break up because little seeds have been planted. Little sparks have ignited a flame, and over time, it grows, and it grows. In many cases, it gets compounded. Especially if comparisons are done on a regular or routine basis. That situation will end up becoming more and more dominant in the relationship. It creates bitterness and anger. It will drive a wedge into a relationship.

Second, don't criticize your wife to others. Criticizing your wife to other people is a very bad thing. I'm around men a lot of times, and I often hear conversations where men are running their wives down. Don't do that to your wife. Don't run her down to other people.

Included in this is that you should never ever criticize your wife to your family. Do you have issues with your wife that need to be talked about? Go get sound, biblical counsel. Don't do it with the family. One day, you're going to forgive your wife and move on from it, but family members will tend to hold onto those things. Don't talk her down in the relationship. Put her first in the relationship, elevate her into a higher position in a relationship, and you will have a stronger relationship.

When we talk about fidelity to your wife, be very cautious about engaging in a relationship with other women. And I'm not talking about a sexual relationship; I'm talking about a relationship where you spend a lot of time talking with them. Never get to the point of spending time alone with them. You're opening a doorway for greater danger to come into a relationship. You're opening a doorway to drive a wedge between you and your wife. So, you have to be very cautious about doing those kinds of things.

Another major issue is the area of pornography. Pornography will destroy a marriage. But pornography is very real in the culture that we live in. Pornography can be seen almost everywhere you look. Even TV programs show what many people refer to as soft porn. The pornography that's available today paints an unrealistic picture of women. It is demeaning to women, and according to the biblical guidance given on the subject, it is straight-up adultery. A relationship with women through pornography is just as much adultery as a physical relationship. Most men don't view it like that, but that's exactly how God views it.

God said that if you look upon another woman with lust in your heart, you have committed adultery. If you have to build barriers around your life to keep yourself from that area, do it. Every person has an element of their personality that is addictive. Everyone has an addiction of some kind, in their life—caffeine, sugar, food, or drugs. The pornography addictions are just as real. And once a person gets into it, they have to learn how to build barriers to keep it away.

Forgiveness

Forgiveness is probably one of the most important areas in marriage. You've got to be willing to forgive each other in a relationship. All unforgiveness does is build walls in your relationship to prevent the intimacy that God wants you to have in that relationship. When you deal with the subject of forgiveness, no one can change a past transgression. There's nothing you can do for something that you've done in the past, other than ask for forgiveness. And so, when you get into arguments, don't bring up past transgressions in the relationship. If you've dealt with that situation, you have to let it go. You've got to move on. One of the qualities of love is that love covers all things.

Most people recognize 1 Corinthians 13, which discusses love. It's frequently read at weddings and quoted in sermons. This chapter gives you some very important guidelines on how to have a loving relationship in the home.

Verse 5 says, *"It [love] does not seek its own, it is not provoked, and it thinks no evil."* A literal understanding of that passage means that love does not keep a record. That's the idea behind it. It does not store up past failures in a relationship. Forgiveness is not excusing what happened. Forgiveness is releasing a person from the debt that you believe they owe you for the hurt they caused in your life. Forgiveness is letting that hurt go, letting that situation go, so healing can take place.

Forgiveness is like removing a thorn. When you remove the thorn, the soreness is still there. But in time, the soreness is going to go away. It's going to ease away. But if you leave that thorn in there, it's going to continue to fester, and it's going to continue to cause problems.

In 1Peter 4, he says, *"And above all things have fervent love for one another."* He's talking about relationships in the Christian life, but this also applies to marriage. Have fervent love for one another, for *love will cover a multitude of sins.*

Isn't covering up sin bad? Covering up sin and your own life is bad because you're supposed to confess your sin. But covering sin in the life of another person simply means that instead of having unforgiveness or harboring anger towards that person, you replace it with love. You cover that hurt with love, and you love that person as an act of your will. So, what you want to do in a marriage relationship is let past transgressions go and move forward in restoring the fire in that relationship.

Anger

This brings us to the issue of anger in a relationship.

Be angry, and do not sin": do not let the sun go down on your wrath, nor give place to the devil.—Ephesians 4:26

How can we be angry and not sin, yet also not let the sun go down on wrath? In the first part of that passage, where he talks about being angry and not sinning, he's talking about God's righteous, proper anger. You should be angry when God is defied. But when we talk about personal anger, personal anger is the decision that we make. Personal anger is a decision that we choose to exercise.

Many times, you'll hear people say someone made them angry. I cannot make anyone angry. You cannot make anyone angry. A person becomes angry because they choose to be angry. You can put the goods out there on the table to provoke someone to anger, but you can't make them choose anger.

He moves on in this passage to say, "Do not let the sun go down on your wrath." What does that tell you? As you go to bed mad, you're going to wake up mad. When you wake up mad, you're going to pour more fuel on the fire and create more problems. I've done that in my relationship. And if I go to bed mad, I wake up mad in the morning.

Put your anger to rest, get rid of it. Find out what the cause is and why you chose to be angry in this situation. 1 Corinthians 13:5 reminds us that love does not behave rudely, and it does not seek its own, and it is not provoked. Love will cover that and keep you from being provoked. Don't allow little things in a relationship to provoke you to anger. When you provoke anger, anger takes over, and then you lose the ability to think rationally and make proper decisions. When you get angry, you will tend to say things and do things that you would never do if you weren't angry. Anger will cause you to lose your discipline as far as your ability and engage in conversation.

So, in a marriage relationship, if there's a little issue, you have to get it out and put it on the table. Put it behind you and don't bring it up anymore. Move forward in the relationship.

The idea behind marriage is that you have to build towards that relationship every day. If you keep planting a bunch of little seeds of problems like unforgiveness, jealousy, and anger, you will harvest those same things.

Scripture is clear that being unforgiving is a sin. Don't ever think sin sits idle. Sin is always progressive. Sin will always take you somewhere where you don't wanna to go. And it will continue to progress. And it will continue to build. And if you harbor unforgiveness in your heart towards your wife, trust me, then unforgiveness is going to turn into a flame.

The same thing is true for the wife. If you provoke the wife, and you keep criticizing or comparing her and belittling her, she's going to get to a point where that stuff's going to build up, and it's going to create problems. Sometimes it's outward problems, sometimes it's inward problems. But she is likely to just pull away. You have to make sure in that relationship that you stay clean and that you don't provide fuel for the fire to create problems with her.

The relationship between husband and wife is a delicate relationship, and it requires both parties to work from both sides. The husband is the head of the wife. That is not to be viewed as some authoritarian position where you rule over the family, and you control everyone's activity. Being head of the family immediately puts you in the same relationship Christ has with the Church. That means you're the head of love, you're the head of all that is good in the home, you're the head of the spiritual temperature of the home, and you're the head of all things that pertain to God. God has put you there as a physical representation of that.

But because of our sin nature, many times as men, we view it from the human perspective. We think, "I'm in charge, I'm in control, and you're going to do what I tell you to do." There is nowhere in the biblical model for a man to be doing that.

Authoritarian rule or tyranny in the home is a direct manifestation of sin in the heart. If you're leading your home like that, you're not leading your home; you're destroying your home because Christ doesn't lead the Church like that. The Bible says, *"Love your wife as Christ loves the Church."*

Look at how He deals with the Church. He's very gracious. He's very kind. He's very long-suffering. Aren't you glad God doesn't just pull the trigger every time you sin and smash you into the ground? God is very gracious to us. God is always building us up, encouraging us. 2 Corinthians 2 reminds us that Christ is always leading us in triumph and victory. He's always leading us in a sweet aroma of His blessings that He provides for us. That is a model of how a wife is to be led in the home. It's a model of how a family should be led in the home. The man sets the temperature, the temperament, and the direction of the home.

In order for that to be done, that man has to have a right relationship with God to begin with, and it has to be a vibrant relationship, like a relationship that is continually fed and a relationship that is continually growing.

Men have a difficult job in a marriage relationship. You battle your own sinfulness all the time. But you have to be careful, lest your sinful nature poison other people. Practice forgiveness, practice fidelity, practice acceptance. Learn to forgive your wife. Learn to be faithful to your wife. The greatest thing you can do in your home is to lead your home, lead your wife, as Christ leads the Church. Grace, humility, kindness, and love that cover a multitude of sin. A home built on love, forgiveness, and commitment between two people is a wonderful thing. And that's what God wants us to do.

CHAPTER 14
The Role of Children
How the Children Function in a Family Unit

Wives, submit to your own husbands, as is fitting in the Lord.

Husbands, love your wives and do not be bitter toward them.

Children, obey your parents in all things, for this is well pleasing to the Lord.

Fathers, do not provoke your children, lest they become discouraged.—Colossians 3:18-21

In this chapter, we're going to look at the role of children in a relationship and our responsibility to children.

Although it seems verse 20 is addressing children, this is really a passage to parents to urge them to teach their children the things of God, so that the children can obey the parents. Children learn the basic instructions within the home that lead them to follow God rather than society and to change society in turn.

Psalm 127:3 refers to children as a heritage from the Lord, as fruit of the womb, and as a reward. Children are a gift from God, and children belong to God. He gives children to parents to bring up in the nurture and admonition to the Lord. The responsibility of parents is to bring their children up to honor God and to fulfill the command to love the Lord your God with all your heart, mind, and soul, and to love your neighbors as yourself. In reality, everything in Scripture feeds into one of those sides. How do I love God, and how do I love my fellow man? That's what parents are supposed to be teaching their children, because your children don't belong to you. They are a gift to you from God, to train, to love, to cherish, and to lead.

It's our responsibility as parents to make sure we're inputting the right information to lead our children to God. We are to provide them with the knowledge so they can love God, they will honor God, they will respect God, but also where they will honor and respect and love other people too. Children do not come with that natural knowledge within them. It has to be instilled there.

Teaching Them to Obey

Children have a command from God to obey their parents. That command is a present imperative. An imperative is a command. The present tense means it's an ongoing thing. In other words, children obey their parents as long as they're in that relationship. Of course, we're to honor our mother and father, but what happens when children get older? There's going to come a time when they're going to leave that home, and the Bible says, *A man shall leave his mother and father and be joined unto his wife* (Genesis 2:24). They start a separate unit. Now they have their own authority structure to bring their children under.

However, as long as children live in your home, they're under the authority of the parents, and it's important to understand that and to realize that. In this passage, the word children there is the word *Tek-'non*. *Tek- 'non* means to bring forth, or in this case, bear children. In the plural form, it means descendants. So, it's a very general word for offspring. The word obey comes from the word obedience, which is the word *hupakoe*; a compound word *hupa* meaning under, and *akoe* meaning to hear. It means to subordinate, to obey, or hearken unto something. Implied in that is that the children have received guidance or are receiving guidance from their parents. And their responsibility is to follow or honor this guidance in all they do.

These passages are very similar to passages in Ephesians. Both show that it's a responsibility of the parents to instruct the children about God, to bring their children up to honor God.

Children, obey your parents in the Lord, for this is right. Honor your father and mother, which is the first commandment with promise, that it may be well with you and you may live long on the earth. And fathers, do not provoke your children to wrath, but bring them up in the training and admonition of the Lord.— Ephesians 6:1-3

What are some common ways that children can be provoked?

Well, one of the very common ways is to control and to be oppressive, but another way to provoke children to wrath is to not provide them with proper guidance for life. Children become very frustrated because children need guidance. Children need proper instruction, and when children are not given proper instruction, it creates frustration in their life. One of the damaging things about sin is, we will promote self and think only of self unless we receive proper instruction. We have an objective basis for this, and that is from our creator, God. God provides us with this instruction for life, and it's the responsibility of the parents to teach the children. Children have to have guidance. One of the problems in the society we live in today is that we have a lot of children who have grown up without instruction and without discipline in their lives, and it's reflected in the culture.

You can look at a lot of the stuff happening in our society, even so far as school shootings and murdering children. I didn't see it when I was in school growing up. When I was in high school, it was a very common practice for us to drive to school. I had a pickup truck, and I drove to school, and I had two items on my gun rack on the truck. I usually had a rifle in there, and underneath that, I had an axe handle for close-quarter work. That's just what we carried as our status symbol.

We weren't planning to go to school and shoot it up. To be honest with you, that idea didn't even enter our minds. We had shooting clubs at the school. Many schools where I grew up had rifle teams. Now, schools are gun-free zones. Why is this kind of stuff happening? We have a generation of provoked young people who have been brought up without proper guidance. They've never had instruction; they've never been taught basic things like manners.

People tend to be angry; people are in a hurry; people are on edge and agitated. People, to a great extent, lack manners, respect, common courtesy, and speak back against authority. When I grew up, it didn't enter my mind to be disrespectful to a teacher.

I've been spanked by neighbors. I'd do something bad with a friend, and their dad would come out, and they'd get a whipping, and I'd get a whipping for being with them. They'd call my parents. I would ask them not to call my dad. I was going to be disciplined twice for that. I didn't want that in my life, so I obeyed. When you don't have that basic discipline in the home, then you don't have discipline for the teachers. Then that flows over to not having respect for your employer, you don't have respect for police officers, law enforcement, laws on the road, and in the community. You produce a lawless society because you plant the seeds of rebellion and anger in a young person as they grow up.

Children have to have instruction. What we're experiencing in our culture today is from a breakdown in the family and basic instructions in the home. It's not going to get better. It's going to get worse because that generation is going to have children, too. And so, we as Christian parents have to instruct our children. You have to guide your children and teach them how to love God and how to love their fellow man.

They learn from your instruction, and they learn from watching you. So, it's going to require you and me as parents to live a life that has character.

Character is extremely important. Who you are, what you do, and how you act around your children—children learn from that, much if not more than what they learn from instruction. Are you polite, kind, and do you live your life filled with the Spirit and guided by the Word of God? The word of God is important because mom follows the Word of God, and the Word of God is important because dad follows the Word of God. You instruct them like that; you bring them up that way. It goes all the way back to the book of Deuteronomy.

Only take heed to yourself, and diligently keep yourself, lest you forget the things your eyes have seen, and lest they depart from your heart all the days of your life. And teach them to your children and your grandchildren, especially concerning the day you stood before the Lord your God in Horeb, when the Lord said to me, 'Gather the people to Me, and I will let them hear My words, that they may learn to fear Me all the days they live on the earth, and that they may teach their children.'—Deuteronomy 4:9-10

Later, in Deuteronomy 6, Israel is urged to love the Lord God with all their hearts and to teach their children the commandments. According to this chapter, we are to do this when we're in our house, when we walk by the way, when we lie down, and when we rise up. Israel bound them as a sign on their hands, and they were on the doorposts of their houses and gates.

He's telling Israel they have a responsibility to honor God first, and then to teach their children to honor God. They would take that Scripture, the Shema, and carry a little box that would have it on their hand, a little leather box, and it would be strapped on their arm, and then they would strap one on their head. The picture is that whatever you think, and then whatever you do with your hand, do it all as unto the Lord. That's exactly what we're learning in the New Testament. It's teaching your children to prioritize their relationship with God, but He gives them specific instructions regarding what to teach them. It is the responsibility of parents to do that.

Back in Colossians 3:20, children are to obey their parents in all things. And then He says, *For this is well pleasing to the Lord.* How do children obey their parents? They obey their parents by submitting to what the parents have taught them. So, if the parents aren't teaching the children, how can the children be pleasing to God? They can't because the parent has to instruct them.

Teaching them to Worship

So, if you want your children to be in a position of pleasing God, you must understand that the worship of God is prescriptive. Worship is not what I decide to present to God; worship is not what you decide to present to God. True worship is presenting to God what God says to present. God tells you how to worship Him. He instructs us how to worship Him. He says to worship in spirit and in truth. You've got to be filled with the Spirit, and you've got to be guided by the Word of God. You've got to speak to God, and sing to God, and pray to God, and talk to God, and receive instruction from God in a manner that God says.

For children to be pleasing to God, they have to have guidelines. And when it comes to worship and pleasing God, there's more to it than what we tend to think. In his confession in Psalm 51, David says, *For you do not desire sacrifice, or else I would give it, you do not delight in burnt offerings. The sacrifices of God are a broken spirit, a broken and a contrite heart. These O God, you will not despise.*

David is saying he could run out and make a sacrifice to God, but God is more concerned about his heart and making sure his heart is right before God.

God is concerned about our hearts. As parents, we have to be concerned about the hearts of our children, that our children look to God, and they honor God, and they respect God, and they love God. And then that will flow into the other relationship, which is with their fellow man. See, one of the problems in our society today is that people hate each other because they don't love God. God tells us that. He says, you can't love your fellow man if you don't love me, and you really can't love me if you don't love your fellow man. Children have to be instructed on this, and that instruction comes from the parents.

You don't have to bring out a 40-pound family Bible. Teach your kids about God when you instruct them in everyday life; relate it back to God.

We serve the Lord, and we worship the Lord. The Lord is primary in our life; He's first place. Why do we pray before meals? God has instructed us to pray, to be thankful for the food we have. Yes, dad worked hard, mom worked hard to provide this food, but God gave us health, God band rought us into favor with the people that hired us. God ultimately brings the resources to us; therefore, we're grateful to God for this, and we're asking God to thank him for our food, protect our food, that we might eat this food so we can better serve God.

You take the everyday moments of life and connect them to God, but to do that, you first need to be right with God yourself. If God isn't a priority in your own life, He won't be a priority in your children's lives either. As parents, it's crucial to understand that our children learn about God by observing us. So how do we make this happen? The Bible provides clear guidelines, emphasizing the importance of training and discipline in raising them in faith.

Teaching Them Through Discipline

Throughout Scripture, we are given clear instructions to provide guidance, insight, knowledge, and wisdom. Proverbs 6:20 advises a son to keep his father's command and not forsake his mother's teaching, emphasizing the importance of the Shema—being aware of God's instructions both day and night. True guidance comes from the Word of God. Children need to learn about authority, and parents must be that authority, exercising it in love. Properly discipling a child is an ongoing process, with discipline serving as a tool for teaching. However, if a child doesn't learn authority, respect cannot follow.

Parents often struggle with consistency—allowing a child to disobey repeatedly until they finally lose their patience and react angrily. From the start, parents need to guide and instruct their children, especially when they're young, as they're more receptive to learning. What works for one child may not work for another, but consistency is key, and children must understand authority. While every child learns differently, parents are responsible for teaching them. This means explaining *why* certain actions are expected, emphasizing that both parent and child are under authority. We serve the same God, and when we teach our children, we must do so with clarity and love, helping them understand that disobedience to God is displeasing to Him.

Rebelling against God carries consequences—a price to pay. As the prophet said in 1 Samuel, rebellion is like the sin of witchcraft. Parental instruction is vital because children won't know right from wrong without it. Parents must provide that guidance. If you don't teach your children to love God, the world will teach them to do the opposite. Someone is always teaching your children, whether you're intentional about it or not.

The Church can provide instruction, but it's not the Church's primary responsibility—it's the parents' responsibility above all else. The same goes for the school; it can support, but the parents must take the lead in guiding their children. This task is vitally important and, more than that, it's commanded by God. It's one of the fundamental responsibilities of parenthood. It's not an easy job, especially when you teach your children the right way. They will constantly face opposition from others trying to steer them in the wrong direction.

If we fail to properly teach and discipline our children, we are cheating them in life and setting them up for failure. As parents, we must take this responsibility seriously. The Word of God commands us to raise our children in the "nurture and admonition of the Lord," which requires sacrifice, time, and intentional effort. When done right, it shows. You can tell when parents are actively training their children in faith and character.

We live in a cruel and vicious world, and many people are growing weary of it. It's crucial that we equip our children to succeed, honor God, and love others. When we do, God promises that it will go well for us and our children.

CHAPTER 15

Provoking Children to Wrath—Pt. I

A Warning to Parents

Now that we've discussed how to instruct children, we'll address provoking children to wrath—or rather, how to avoid doing just that.

In Ephesians 6:21, similar to our verses in Colossians, Paul says, *"Fathers do not provoke your children lest they become discouraged."* The idea of the father is that God has placed a father in a position of headship in a home. Therefore, what goes on in a home should be directed through the fathers, but in the Greek, it's speaking of mom and dad. Why? Because parents make up a team to work within a family. That's how God designed it. A husband and wife are partners in the relationship to lead their children to love God and to lead their children to rightly relate to their fellow man, and to have a peaceful society.

In this verse, what does the word provoke mean? The Greek word for provoke comes from *Erethizo.* The root word is *Eretho,* which means to stir to anger or to exasperate. Some Bibles translate it as exasperate. It means to arouse a person or excite a person in a bad way, to stir them up to anger.

With children, when parents create that environment, they can provoke that child. They can create an environment where that child will bring out anger, and they will be extremely upset.

We're going to look at some areas where parents can provoke children to anger. Parenting is one of the most difficult tasks in the world. Until you go to the scriptures, you have no instruction manual. But God gives us some very good guidelines on how to bring up children. Many people view the Bible as being antiquated and out of date when it comes to things such as this. I yield to society. Look at society and tell me if we've learned a lot, or is society in general getting better, or do you see society in general getting worse? Do you see people becoming better in relationships, or do you see people who tend to become worse? We need to go back to a biblical model.

As a part of that, we must parent as Scripture teaches and avoid provoking our children to anger. There are many ways that a child can be provoked to anger.

Overprotection Provokes Anger

The Lord doesn't shield us from every setback. Though God could prevent all failure, doing so would keep us from developing resilience and wisdom. Without the opportunity to fail, we'd struggle to mature and learn in meaningful ways.

God sets clear guidelines for us to follow, and when we fail to follow them, we face consequences. Sometimes, God chastens us by allowing us to experience the natural outcomes of our choices. In the same way, parents must be cautious not to shield their children from every mistake, as failure teaches important lessons. Overprotecting children from failure prevents them from learning valuable life skills and understanding the consequences of their actions.

Giving every child a participation trophy can send the message that effort doesn't matter and that everyone deserves the same reward regardless of their contribution. This can lead to complacency, where children come to believe that success is guaranteed, no matter how hard they work. As a result, the prize loses its meaning.

Failure, on the other hand, often drives us to try harder and put forth more effort. One of the most valuable lessons children can learn is that failure isn't the end—it's simply an event, not an identity. In the real world, everyone faces setbacks, and how we respond to them defines our growth. I always tell people that a person's true character shows when they don't get a promotion. Do they get back to work and continue to perform well, or do they become bitter? The first person is the one you want on your team.

Allowing children to experience failure is essential for their growth, but it's important that they understand failure doesn't define them. Instead, failure is an opportunity to learn, improve, and ultimately succeed. When parents prevent failure out of overprotection, it can hinder a child's development and breed frustration. Children need to face challenges and setbacks in order to fully engage with life and build resilience.

The next issue that can provoke a child to anger is excessive or incorrect discipline or no discipline at all. Children need to have guidelines.

Incorrect Discipline Provokes Anger

Now, what do I mean by incorrect discipline?

Incorrect discipline is disciplining a child when you're angry or mad. You need to, as a parent, step away from the issue and calm down. When you discipline a child, you have to instruct the child also. Discipline always comes with instruction, according to Proverbs

29:15. It says the *"rod and reproof give wisdom."* This verse means corporal punishment, and it means discipline, but it also has instruction with it. A child has to clearly understand why they're being disciplined.

The second thing about disciplining a child is that a child needs to learn discipline at the earliest age possible. Discipline should be very minimal, but it should be enough to let a child understand there are consequences. I'm not talking about being cruel or beating children. I'm talking about applying a little pain to the situation because pain is a powerful motivator. That makes some people uncomfortable, but I'm here to tell you that pain is a powerful motivator in a child. I'm not talking about excessive pain. I'm talking about enough where they understand, "Wow, I shouldn't do that." When a child is young and they learn that, it often doesn't have to be a lot of physical discipline after that because the child understands the consequences of

Failure to obey leads to the natural consequence of needing correction. Children must learn to respect authority and understand that there are consequences for their actions. Physical discipline, when necessary, should always be done in private and with instruction. The child must understand *why* they are being disciplined, so the lesson is clear. Proverbs 29:17 says, *"Correct your son, and He will give you rest; yes, He will give delight to your soul."* Without discipline, children can become frustrated, as they don't understand the boundaries that should guide their behavior.

Children are born with a sinful nature (Psalm 51:5), and you don't have to teach them to lie, be selfish, or be rude. These behaviors come naturally. That's why they need guidelines—clear expectations about what is acceptable and what is not. For example, there are ways we behave in certain situations: how we act at the dinner table, how we speak to others, and how we treat people in general. A child's behavior must align with these guidelines if they are to grow into respectful, responsible individuals.

Why are guidelines essential? Because children, like adults, have a sinful nature, and without boundaries, they will struggle to navigate life's challenges. Just as God gave His law to the children of Israel to guide them (Galatians 3:24), parents must establish rules to teach children right from wrong. God's law covers two key relationships: our relationship with Him and with others. The Great Commandment sums it up in Matthew 22:37-39: *"You shall love the Lord your God with all your heart, with all your soul, and with all your mind... You shall love your neighbor as yourself."* Similarly, children must learn to love and respect both God and others, and clear guidelines are the way to help them do so.

Children, in the same way, need to have basic guidelines so they understand where they can operate. That's got to be clearly explained and clearly understood by the children. They need to understand that there are consequences when they violate the guidelines. Why? When they get out of the house and violate guidelines, the consequences are a whole lot bigger. Life is full of guidelines, and where a child learns that is in the house. They learn how to honor God in their life, how to love God in their life, and how to love their fellow man. So, excessive discipline, incorrect discipline, or no discipline will create anger in a child.

Finding Fault Provokes Anger

Number three is constantly finding fault in a child. It's another area that's very bad. If we look at the friends of Job in the Old Testament, we see the anger that is aroused when people constantly find fault, even fault that doesn't exist. These friends of Job are accusing Job without a legitimate reason.

When we raise children or bring children up in the nurture and admonition of the Lord, constantly finding fault with a child will create anger. It will tear that child down. Blaming without a clear purpose towards progress is not good. Whenever you critique a child, you have to have a reason for it. You can't do it just to provoke or belittle to child, because by doing that, you're going to create anger in a child. Don't find unnecessary fault with the child.

God loves me and God loves you in spite of imperfections. Every person is different. None of us is perfect, and children are not perfect. And children will rarely live up to the standard that you have. Don't do that to a child. If you have to correct a child, give them the reason. But don't just find fault because you believe there's fault. That's what Job's friends were doing. They were accusing Job of all kinds of stuff that Job hadn't done. Children are the same way, and it will create anger in them.

A Lack of Consistency Provokes Anger

Number four is the lack of consistency in discipline. Consistency is often one of the hardest aspects of parenting, but it is essential. There are two key areas where consistency is needed. The first is in how you apply discipline. If a child breaks a rule, you cannot simply overlook it. You must stop and address the issue immediately. Ignoring a violation only sends the message that the rule doesn't really matter. Consistency means that when a rule is broken, there is a clear, predictable consequence every time, so the child understands that boundaries are firm and consequences are real.

Another area where consistency can be lacking is when the parents aren't on the same page. One parent might be strict, while the other doesn't enforce any rules. It's important for both parents to agree on how to discipline, what the boundaries are, and how they're going to handle things. Once you've agreed, it's crucial to stick to it so the child knows what to expect. If there's disagreement between the parents, it only creates confusion and makes it harder for the child to understand what's expected of them.

Children have to see that there's consistency between the parents, and there's consistency whenever a guideline is broken. Failing to provide consistency creates confusion and will provoke a child to anger.

My brethren, count it all joy when you fall into various trials, knowing that the testing of your faith produces patience. But let patience have its perfect work, that you may be perfect and complete, lacking nothing. If any of you lacks wisdom, let him ask of God, who gives to all liberally and without reproach, and it will be given to him. But let him ask in faith, with no doubting, for he who doubts is like a wave of the sea driven and tossed by the wind. For let not that man suppose that he will receive anything from the Lord; he is a double-minded man, unstable in all his ways.—James 1:2-8

The immediate context of that verse deals with the person going through trials. That person asks God, but he doesn't believe God's going to do it. That's instability. God says, "If you're going to ask, you have to believe that I'm going to do it. You have to ask in faith." But the principle in that text is that when you don't have a standard, you create instability, and instability creates double-mindedness. Parents have to be consistent with each other and have to be consistent with discipline.

Comparison Provokes Anger

Number five is comparing your children to others. Do not compare your children to other children. 2 Corinthians 10 talks to the Church at Corinth about the dangers of comparing yourself to others. Paul says, *"For we dare not class ourselves or compare ourselves with those who commend themselves."* Paul is saying, "You think you're okay, because you're comparing yourself to somebody else."

When you compare a child to other children, or worse yet, compare them to their siblings, that does several things. It devalues the fact that everyone is unique and different. Without realizing it, what a parent is trying to do is make everyone the same. But also comparing them like that creates resentment between siblings. It will reach the point where they dislike that other sibling.

When you compare children, it frustrates a child. When you frustrate that child, it will create anger in that child. Be consistent, be fair, and don't compare them.

God is pretty consistent. God is definitely not overprotective. He's not excessive, nor does He ever use incorrect discipline, nor does He ever skip discipline. God doesn't find fault in us, and God doesn't compare us to other people. So, if we're going to be a Godly parent, we have to follow a Godly model. If you will learn to discipline and to train up your children with humility and mercy, and think about yourself in the process, you will do well.

Parenting is a learning process. You learn as you go. Children do not come with an instruction manual, but you have the Word of God, and the Word of God is sound, the Word of God is true, and Word of God will endure forever. The grass can wither, and the flowers fade away, but the Word of God is going to breathe forever. Stick with the Word of God, and you will be safe.

Deal with your children the way God deals with you. Fair, consistent, and very merciful. Our God is very merciful in the way He deals with us. He doesn't crush us. He doesn't break us. He deals in His kind, gentle manner. He says in the eleventh chapter of Matthew, "Come unto me all you who labor and are heavy laden, and I will give you rest. For my burden is light and I care about you." And that is a good model for parents.

Parents have to care. Parents have to be kind. Parents have to be merciful. You're bringing up a person who is going to be an effective part of society, and you want to make sure you provide proper guidance for them.

CHAPTER 16
Provoking to Wrath—Pt. II
What Children Need from a Parent

In this chapter, we'll continue looking at what it means to provoke a child to wrath and how we can avoid it. The passage in Ephesians says, *Fathers do not provoke your children to wrath, but bring them up in the nurture and admonition of the Lord* (Ephesians 6:4).

We have clear instructions in this sister book to Colossians. Here, we're going to cover six more areas where we need to be wary of provoking our children to wrath. This kind of stuff is not a pleasant topic for parents, but by hearing this, many times it brings to light things you're not aware of, and it will help us to change. Bringing up children will change you as a person, because now you're having to instruct another human and you're having to be an example for them, and it really challenges you in your own personal walk.

Remember that your children belong to God. Children, the Bible says, are a heritage from the Lord. They're given to us as gifts, but they belong to God because all children are accountable to God, just like all adults are accountable to God. It says, God has put upon the parent the responsibility to bring God's children up in the direction that God

wants them to go, in the pathway that God wants them to walk. As
parents, we are molding and shaping the next generation of believers
in the Church. And so, we have specific guidelines from God on how
we're supposed to do this. If we fail at this, in essence, we're neglecting
God's children, and God is not pleased by that.

In this verse from Ephesians, the Bible is assuming that this provoking behavior is common. We have to protect against it. We have to
be sensitive to it. That's one of the reasons you have a husband and wife
in a Christian family. They check and balance. One gets out of line,
or is not going right, the other one's there to help guide and direct,
because a husband and wife are a team. They work together and they
are working together to bring these children up the right and proper
way.

The first issue we will look at today is neglecting time with children. That is an easy way to provoke a child to wrath. Deuteronomy 6
tells us the importance of time in instructing a child in truth. The New
Testament version says to bring them up in the nurture and admonition of the Lord. Admonition has to do with correction. When they
get out of line, nurture means to bring up food. Well, what's the food
that you bring your child up with? They need physical food, but they
also need spiritual food, and so it's up to the parent to bring them up
with the right spiritual nutrition. Many times, we make excuses for not
knowing this or for neglecting to do it. We have excuses like, "I don't
have time based on my job, I need time for myself, I need rest, I need
to serve in other areas, and I need to have time with my wife." But no
excuse takes the place of what God has commanded us to do.

Children are to be a priority in life, not an add-on. You have to
learn to sacrifice time to spend time with your children. Neglecting
children creates anger in the children. So, let's look at what is some
practical ways that you can spend some time with your child.

Pray with your child when you're in a car sing with your child. Memorize Bible verses with your child, serve others with your child, and let them be a part of that. An important time to spend with your children would be at supper time or at breakfast, and spend time with those children without the TV. Spend time talking to them, getting feedback from them, asking them about how their life is going, and what's happening in their life, and what's going on in their life. Let them share what has taken place in their life. And then, as they do that, it opens doorways for you to provide instruction, with just probing questions like, "Well, how did that make you feel when that person said that to you? What was your reaction to that? How did you treat them after that?" Use those opportunities to get your instruction in.

When I talk about teaching children, I'm not talking about dragging a big Bible out and laying it on the coffee table and making the kids sit down to go over a Bible lesson. Just make it practical. Learn how to interact and interject things in a day-to-day conversation. Another good thing to do is set aside one night a week for family night. When our children were young, we did this quite often. You can play sports or board games, and do things that engage the family. Beware if the personalities in the family are extremely competitive, but that's an instructional opportunity for you to guide them out of that mindset. Just spend time as a family.

Devoting time specifically to your children is valuable. If you have to work around the house, a good way to make work much more enjoyable is to bring all the children along and engage in a conversation with them. I would do that quite often with my children while they were growing up. Make time for your children to talk and pray, and to speak with them.

Second, listen to your children when they speak. Proverbs 18:13

says, *he who answers a matter before he hears it, it is folly and shame to him.* You have to learn to listen and to hear what someone is saying. Children are no different.

Telling children things such as "not now" or not devoting time to listen will create the idea that *dad doesn't listen to me.* But what it really communicates is, "My dad doesn't care about me. I'm not important to my dad." When you listen to a child, you're telling that child you care about them, they are important to you, and you love them. That's what you're telling them through nonverbal communication. Just sit there and listen to that child.

When you speak to a child or when you're listening to a child, make eye contact with that child. Look at them. If you're reading a book, put the book down. If you're on your phone, set the phone down and look at the child eye to eye. That's instructional, because it teaches the child, when you engage in conversation, you give full attention to that person.

We want people to listen to us when we talk, and children are no different. Listening to your child when they speak, once again, opens the doorway to greater conversation. But if you're not listening to your child, you're not getting really any realistic feedback from their life about what's going on. So, you need to sit down and listen to them and hear them out. Hear what they have to say and engage in it when they talk. Look at them, and then probe the things that they say.

Number three, we provoke by breaking promises to children. Breaking promises to children will create anger within that child. Matthew 5:37 tells us to let our yes be yes, and let our no be no. What does it mean when Jesus says that? If you promise to do something for somebody, do it. Many times, promises are made to children as a means to manipulate that child into doing certain things. If you do this, we'll do this for you, or if you do that, I'll get this for you. If you make a promise to a child, it's on you to make good on that promise. Because when you fail to fulfill a promise to a child, it creates frustration in that child.

One of the most common ways for unforgiveness to come up in a person's life is that expectations in life are not met through experiences. You have an expectation that somebody is going to do something, and they don't do it. When they don't measure up to that standard, it creates debt. It creates a situation in life where you resent that person. The easiest way to fix it is to stop putting expectations on people. If you go around in your life with expectations of what people are going to do, that they're going to treat you nice and be kind, you'd better get ready. When they don't fulfill that, you're going to have resentment for that person, because you put expectations on them.

When you make a promise to a child, you're loading that child with expectations. They're going about doing what they're doing, thinking about what you promised, and then if you don't fulfill that promise, the end result will be unforgiveness. You've created a situation where that child will have unforgiveness. If you make a promise, come through with it. The best thing is not to make a promise. You train that child up in such a way that when you tell them to do something, you don't have to front-load it with promises. You just tell them, you need to clean your room, versus if you clean your room, I'll take you to get an ice cream. Bribes are not good because something else might come up, and you may not be able to take them. That teaches a child that parents don't keep their word. They don't tell the truth. This creates resentment in them. The best thing to do is just tell them to do something. Then, when they do it, give them a reward for it, if that's what you desire to do. But front-loading a situation with a promise and failing to keep that promise creates resentment in children.

The number four area to be wary of is showing favor to one child over the others. If you have more than one child, favoring one child over the other is a huge risk.

My brethren, do not hold the faith of our Lord Jesus Christ, the Lord of glory, with partiality. For if there should come into your assembly a man with gold rings, in fine apparel, and there should also come in a poor man in filthy clothes, and you pay attention to the one wearing the fine clothes and say to him, "You sit here in a good place," and say to the poor man, "You stand there," or, "Sit here at my footstool," have you not shown partiality among yourselves, and become judges with evil thoughts? —James 2:1-4

It's a very common thing in churches, where people who have money, or popularity, or importance, are favored over others. James said that's not how it's supposed to be done. You're not supposed to show partiality. So, the principle is true. When a family is in a home, do not show favoritism to one child over another. There are ample examples in the Bible.

Now Israel loved Joseph more than all his children, because he was the son of his old age. Also, he made him a tunic of many colors. But when his brothers saw that their father loved him more than all his brothers, they hated him and could not speak peaceably to him. —Genesis 37:3-4

The passage goes on to show how his brothers envied him, but his father kept the matter in mind. In verse 19, we see the plot to kill Joseph because of his dreams and how he is favored. Ultimately, he isn't killed by his brothers, and God does an amazing work of family redemption. But first, his brothers sold him as a slave and pretended he was killed by a wild beast. Their father grieved the loss of his favorite son, which likely only made them happier in their bitterness.

Jacob learned this behavior from his dad. If you remember, Jacob's brother, Esau, was favored by his father, and Jacob was favored by his mother. This created conflict in that relationship. Showing favoritism to children is not a good thing. All children are different, and no two children are going to be the same. The likes and dislikes of one child will most likely not be the likes and dislikes of another child. Each child is created differently, created the way God wanted to create them. They are given to us to bring up properly.

So, what you have to do as a parent is recognize the differences between children, and recognizing differences is something that's good and not bad. It's not something to be criticized because those children are so different. The person who needs to change is *me* when it comes to that. Quit trying to make all your children the same.

If you spend time with one child, make sure you spend time with the other. Make time for all of them and don't create conflict in the family, because that conflict will end up coming out and going through life.

Favoritism creates animosity. Don't make favorites out of children.

The next warning against provoking is scolding or punishing in public. There are times when you have to get on that kid right then and there. For example, if a child runs out into the street, snatch and hold that kid. Walk them back over to you and scold them or give them a swat. That's understandable. What I'm talking about with this point is that when it comes time to discipline that child, if you discipline them in public, it creates embarrassment for the child, and that's not the purpose of discipline. The purpose of discipline is to correct the pathway that the child is on.

Lord, do not rebuke me in your wrath nor chasten me in your hot displeasure.—Psalm 38:1

That was David's prayer to God. He is saying, *God, have mercy on me. Be gentle with me, God.*

That's how we should be with our children. Our motto for life is going to be to deal with our children as God deals with us as His children. God is very merciful, and God is very kind. Rarely does God give us what we deserve in life, and we need to understand that.

When it comes time to discipline a child, you need to take that child in private. There are multiple reasons for this. You never discipline a child without letting them know full well why they're being disciplined. You need to sit down, set that child down, and explain to them why they are being disciplined. The second thing is you never discipline a child in anger. Many times, you have to step back from that situation, calm down, and settle your anger. You have to be under the control of the Spirit when you do that. Don't discipline in anger, and don't discipline without a clear understanding of why they're being disciplined. Make sure the discipline is appropriate to the offense that was committed. But to scold, shame, or publicly embarrass that child is not productive in the life of that child, and they will get to where they resent that.

Most children will take discipline if it's done properly. If it's done improperly, they're going to be very distasteful towards it.

The last warning is modeling unchristian behavior in front of your children. That will provoke anger in a child. If you're cursing around your children or yelling at your spouse, that is not good. That is not productive in a situation where you're bringing up children. If you're faking your Christian walk, and you're putting on the fake smile, and have fake actions, children can see through that real quick. If you're going to live well before your children, you have to set an example before them. One of the fundamental marks of a leader is that you set the example.

In other words, if you don't allow something in the life of your child, don't do it yourself. Be consistent in how you live before your children. Children will grow up thinking that if mom and dad get angry, God must be angry. Children relate a lot of what they think about God to the way their parents react with each other. Children learn how to solve conflict by watching their parents. They watch how their parents are handling issues. They learn how to treat other people by how their parents treat each other and by how they interact with each other. They learn consistency in their Christian walk by watching how consistency is modeled in the lives of their parents.

Children learn far more from what they see than what they hear. It's important that, as a parent, you do not model un-Christ-like behavior in front of your child. If they often see you boiling over with rage, they don't want anything to do with your faith when they get out of your home. You have to be careful with that because you should be setting a positive example before your children. Setting the example is one of the most critical things in bringing up children. When we fail to be consistent in this area, it creates great anger within a child.

The thing about bringing up children is that you also have to bring up children with humility and grace in their lives. Let them realize that when they mess up, they can patch it up. And when you mess up with them, go to that child and admit to them that you were wrong. When parents are humble before their children, children can receive that, and they need to know that. That's instructive too.

When I do something that's displeasing, I have a responsibility to fix that. Let me show you how I can fix it. I need grace and forgiveness in my life every day, just like everyone else does, and just like you do.

Deal with your child in that manner. But if you're harsh, over-bearing, and forceful, it's going to create hostility with those children. You've got to be consistent. We have instructions from God to bring children up in a nurture and admonition of the Lord, and that means we're meant to model before our children how God deals with us.

God gives us an opportunity to start fresh all the time. If we need to start fresh with our children, now is the time to do so. We're going to do it right. You have to be open and communicate that to your children, because you want your children to grow up to love you, but you also want them to grow up and love God. It's parents who are bringing up the next generation, and it's very important as parents that we model consistency and stay as true to the Word of God as we can in all that we do.

CHAPTER 17
The Family as a Whole
Who We Are in Christ

Wives, submit to your own husbands, as is fitting in the Lord.

Husbands, love your wives and do not be bitter toward them.

Children, obey your parents in all things, for this is well pleasing to the Lord.

Fathers, do not provoke your children, lest they become discouraged.—Colossians 3:18-21

What is a family supposed to look like? What is a marriage meant to look like?

The key to marriage is not necessarily finding the right mate but being the right mate. The focus should be on yourself. It should be on what we need to do to be better. Marriage is defined in Scripture as a covenant relationship. It's an agreement made between two people, or a contract. The contract between them is also before God, where vows and a ring are exchanged. A ring is symbolic of the covenant. Marriage is an agreement between a husband and wife, and God established the first marriage in the Bible when He brought Adam and Eve together. He actually brought Eve to Adam after He had created her out of Adam, and God gave him a specific responsibility. He said, "It's not good that man should be alone." So, He made a helper comparable to him. He put them together, and they became a leadership team. They had a specific responsibility, as shown in Genesis 1 and 2.

He made them to manage or be stewards over His creation. You are in a position of authority. You have dominion, you have rule, you have responsibility, and God expects us to fulfill that. Man and woman were placed in the garden by God for a specific purpose, and that was to lead and manage God's creation. He turned authority over to them.

We know the whole story. They succumb to a temptation, and they violate the commandment of God. Sin enters the picture and, therefore, what God had created as a unified, harmonious relationship, all of a sudden becomes wrecked. It becomes damaged. And there are two serious things that affect every marriage. The first one is that because of the fall, every person is sinful. The Bible says that all have sinned and come short of the glory of God. It is something we all possess. Sin causes us to look to self. That is the essence of sin itself. So instead of being a harmonious team, each person in that relationship, husband and wife, looks to their self. They look for their own well-being.

The second thing in the relationship is that, as a result of man's sin, God put conflict between the man and the woman in the relationship as a constant reminder of the gravity of sin. We see that in Genesis 3:16. He says to the woman, *I will greatly multiply your sorrow and your conception; in pain, you will bring forth children; your desire will be for your husband, and he shall rule over you.*

We studied the word *desire*. This is sin's desire to control or dominate their life, as is used between Cain and Abel. In a marriage relationship, when you put a husband and wife together in a union, there's an inborn natural desire for the woman to control the husband. But it says, *he shall rule over you*. So, there's a desire for the man to rule that woman or dominate that woman.

Each person is sinful, so they look for their own well-being, instead of leading the family to take dominion over the creation and bringing their children up to understand and know God. The result of sin in marriage is that man and woman both seek their own desire, instead of the desire of God. Instead of managing the creation, they want to manage each other. What God does in salvation is bring you into a relationship with Him, but He also brings your human spirit alive. His Spirit comes to reside within you, but positionally, you are placed in Christ.

We must stop having a self-centered, selfish focus. Deal with people with humility, kindness, and one of the key phrases, forgiveness.

God also deals with the natural animosity that exists in a relationship. When God established marriage in the Bible, you see that God is the author of marriage.

In our culture today, there's a great debate over what marriage is. There's a great debate over what a male is. What a female. The insanity of sin has so invaded our culture that even those who are called by the name of Christ are confused and resist taking a stand for what is the truth. When God created marriage, He said marriage is between a male and a female. Anything less than that is presumption. It's chaos. It is man trying to re-order the divine system that was established by God. Our culture has so embraced that, it's a literal fulfillment of prophetic literature in the Bible, where it talks about a day that is coming when good will be called evil and evil be called good. And that's what you're seeing vomited out on our culture today.

Sin has reached so deeply into our culture in society that we've seen an utter disintegration of the family in front of our very eyes. And yet, people are fearful to stand for the truth of God's Word. God told us there would come a day when that would be the case. God gives us clear outlines and guidance and Scripture for how to put the family back together.

Men and women both need to understand their specific roles and what they do with their family because they're bringing up the next generation. You're bringing up the next generation, and marriage and parenthood, and the family is woven deep in leadership. You've got to lead. What do you lead against? You're leading against the darkness of sin that seeks the corrupt, not just individuals, but an entire culture that we live in. And it takes a unified front to stand against sin.

Wives, recognize your call to submit to your own husband. This means to respect and honor your husband instead of trying to control and dominate his life. Recognize his position and support him, come alongside him as the woman was designed to do in the first place. Being a helpmeet for that man is a compliment, not a hindrance.

A husband, likewise, has a call to love his wife. As a husband and wife, you are, first and foremost, brother and sister in Christ. That comes before the role situation. You're to deal with each other in kindness, goodness, mercy, and forgiveness.

Throughout this book, we've talked about the five critical things that a man has to do in a marriage relationship. He has to lead, to have a presence in a relationship, make provision for the wife, protect the wife, and be the foothold for a promise of good in that relationship. Love your wife as Christ loved the Church. A husband's love for his wife is to be sacrificial. So, he puts himself second; he puts the wife first.

The husband's responsibility is to minister to the wife. The wife's responsibility is to minister to the husband. The wife tries to make the husband the best he can be, and her husband seeks to make the wife the best she can be. The essence of sin in that relationship is that the wife wants to control or change the husband, and the husband wants to dominate the wife. When you see that in a relationship, you're seeing an outworking of sin.

But when you see a wife supporting the husband and the husband supporting the wife, you start seeing a unified relationship. This is something that takes work because we're not naturally that way. Get the focus off of selfishness.

Then Scripture says for children to obey their parents and that father should not provoke their children, lest they become discouraged. The responsibility in a home is for the mother and father to train the children and bring them up to know, and understand, and love God. This idea is not unique to the New Testament. It goes all the way back to the Old Testament.

Psalm 127 describes children as being a blessing, that the man with a quiver full is happy.

And yet, we listen to many people in society today, and when you mention children and it's like they hate their children. All children are such a drain or such a pain.

We must take the role of leadership. Start leading your family and quit letting your kids lead you. That's the truth of Scripture. Even as Christians, we many times reverse the order God says. They see children as an inconvenience. But Israel was called to raise their children in the Word of God. And the whole idea is to train your children to know the Lord and to love the Lord. That's what our responsibility is.

In order to do that, the husband and wife have to model a unified relationship to those children, and they have to bring those children up in the nurture and admonition of the Lord. What is the most important thing to teach your children as they are growing up? The most important thing to teach your children is character.

People don't understand what true Christian character is. Basic things like responsibility, loyalty, and honesty are fundamentals of life. This is what parents should be teaching their children.

Teach your children about God and tell them we are created in the image and likeness of God. Teach them that we are to evidence the character of God in our lives. Demonstrate meekness, long-suffering, kindness, goodness, and all these biblical traits.

As humans, we fail every day, but the idea is humility and forgiveness. Children should learn that a mistake is not final.

We can be a unified front. Children learn that through instruction, and they learn it through their parents.

18.4 million children, that's one out of four children in America, live and grow up without a biological father, a stepfather, or an adoptive father at home.[2] One out of four children. You can add that to roughly one to two out of four children who grow up with fathers that are not teaching their children the Word of God. Most likely, less than one-fourth of all the children in our nation are receiving instruction about their relationship with God and how we're to live before God.

What's the result of a fatherless home? Four times greater risk of poverty, according to the National Fatherhood Initiative[3]. They are more likely to have behavioral problems. They have two times greater risk of infant mortality, are more likely to go to prison, and are more likely to commit a crime. I've been working in prison long enough to know we're seeing fourth-generation people coming into the prison. *Yeah, my daddy did time, my granddaddy did time.* One thing we're

---

[2] National Fatherhood Initiative, *Father Absence Statistics,* accessed September 25, 2025, https://www.fatherhood.org/father-absence-statistic

[3] National Center for Fathering, *The Consequences of Fatherlessness,* accessed September 25, 2025, https://fathers.com/the-consequences-of-fatherlessness/

trying to teach in the prison system now is to give these men and women the basics to break that cycle in the family. We want them to stop that cycle, the cycle of heartache, the cycle of loneliness, and the cycle of hopelessness that prevails in that culture.

Women who grow up in a fatherless home are seven times more likely to become pregnant as a teen. That's a significant figure. They are more likely to face abuse and neglect, and more likely to abuse drugs and alcohol. They are two times more likely to suffer obesity, two times more likely to drop out of school. What does that tell you? Family is very, very important. These are secular statistics that were gathered by secular organizations that are looking and seeing we're in trouble. Something has to change. Something has got to turn around.

God has given us the instruction. And with the Word of God, we have hope. Continue to work with your family. Continue to work with your children, continue to pound into them the truth about God, their relationship with God, and their responsibility to God. Build character in your family and help your children become strong. Give them the tools necessary to face the world that they're going to live in and to be successful in the world.

All you have to do is look at people in Scripture. Daniel grew up in a godless culture. Many people in the Bible, especially the Old Testament prophets, grew up in godless cultures, and yet they were able to live for God and see God work in their lives. If we as parents don't give our children the basics for that, then we don't have hope for that in the future.

With God, there's hope. There's not going to be hope in this world. You're not going to see it fixed. The government is not going to fix it. The government is not going to solve the problem. The one thing that is going to solve the problem is God, and the way He is going to solve it in families is for moms and dads to take back the reins of leadership in their home and bring their children up in the nurture and admonition of the Lord.

Husbands, love your wife as Christ loves the Church. Wives, respect your husband. Children, obey your parents (Ephesians 5:25-6:1). All these little basic fundamentals are so critical to the society and culture that we live in. Paul says God has created in you the ability, through the new birth, to not live under the power of sin and to sacrifice your own desires for the desires of the person that you're married to. Instead of changing God's order, we need to get busy with God's order and move forward with it. God's plan will endure. The Bible tells us the grass will wither, and the flower will fade away, but the Word of God is going to abide forever.

That means that it doesn't matter how bad the culture, society, and everything gets around you, the Word of God is going to be true. If you heed the Word of God, you're walking the right pathway. My encouragement to you as parents is to walk that pathway and do what's right, even if nobody else around you is doing it. Do what the Scripture says. God honors faithfulness in the lives of His people. You need the blessing of God on your home and your family. The blessing of God will be on your home and family if you heed the Word of God. So, keep moving forward, and be successful. But most of all, be faithful in all that you do.

www.ingramcontent.com/pod-product-compliance
Lightning Source LLC
Chambersburg PA
CBHW060023100426
42740CB00010B/1576